BE A WRITING MACHINE 2

Write Faster and Smarter, Beat Writer's Block, and Be Prolific

M.L. RONN

Contents

What You'll Learn from
This Book

When I wrote *Be a Writing Machine* in 2018, I had no idea the book would be so popular. I was just documenting my process of being prolific because I received a lot of questions about it. Plus, writing the book was good therapy for me.

The book has helped writers around the world write faster and smarter, beat writer's block, and be prolific. For some, *Be a Writing Machine* has become a lifestyle.

I've spoken to crowds of over 1,000 people on how to improve your writing speed. I have spoken at the biggest writing conferences in the world, such as 20Books Vegas, Inkers Con, and Writer's Digest. I even wrote an article in *Writer's Digest* about productivity. I've been a guest on some of the biggest indie author podcasts in the world, including "The Self-Publishing Show" and "The Creative Penn." I have also done countless virtual presentations on *Be a Writing Machine* for virtual conferences and writers' groups.

Writers all over the world have emailed me and told me how helpful my advice has been. One author even told me that the book saved them from suicide. I continue to be humbled by how far and wide that little book has traveled.

I have learned so much about productivity since writing the

first *Be a Writing Machine* that I decided to write a sequel. These methods have helped me consistently write at least 10 books per year, grow my writing career, and reach levels of productivity that I only dreamed of previously.

When you write 80+ books, you learn things. Every book teaches you a different lesson. I'd like to share those lessons with you.

A Little About Me

If there is anyone who should *not* have a writing career, it's me.

I built a writing career while raising a family, working full-time, and attending law school classes in the evenings. (I finally graduated in 2021.)

Since the first *Be a Writing Machine*, it has gotten both easier and harder for me to write. I've had to refine my techniques.

My daughter was four years old in 2018. Now she is in elementary school with a schedule full of activities—and I'm the Dad taxi service.

I graduated from law school but became an executive at a global insurance company, making my work schedule even crazier.

My wife suffers from long COVID and a difficult chronic illness that often pulls me away from my writing.

Yet, because of the techniques I will cover in this book, I've managed to keep publishing at least 10 books per year. In fact, my writing speed has gotten *faster* since 2018.

As I said, if there is anyone who should *not* have a writing career, it's me, yet I've persevered. I hope that will make this book's advice more valuable.

A Quick Overview of This Book's Structure

. . .

This book builds on the concepts from the first book.

In *Be a Writing Machine*, I covered mindset, tools, time management, writing smart, and writer's block.

This book follows the same structure.

- The **Mindset** chapter will give you some new ways of thinking about writing and productivity that will help you break past plateaus. To be truly prolific is to see the world of writing in ways that others do not. This chapter will help you do that.
- The **Practical Tools** chapter will give you tips you can use to master new writing methods.
- The **Time Management** chapter will teach you how to cut a hole in the time-space continuum and get more out of your writing time.
- The **Writing Even Smarter** chapter will give you strategies you can apply when you sit down in the chair and begin writing. This is where the real warfare begins, and I'll help you win.
- The **Writer's Block** section will give you some advanced strategies to ensure the words keep flowing 24/7/365.

As I wrote in the first *Be a Writing Machine*: "Remember, prolific isn't just about writing one book fast. It's about producing book after book after book, rain or shine, no matter what. It's about learning how to be systematic."

This book will not only help you build on the concepts from the first *Be a Writing Machine*, but it will also help you reach new heights.

Read on if you're ready to roll back the curtain and explore the beautiful wonders that being prolific will open you to.

Mindset: The Next Levels

I promise this isn't your typical mindset chapter. Just like last time, there is no "woo woo" stuff here. Only practical tips to help you think about productivity in new ways.

So much about writing is mindset-driven, but early in your career, the real challenge is winning the war against yourself. The first *Be a Writing Machine* focused on helping you beat self-doubt so that you can win that war. I'm going to assume that you are fighting that good fight and that you have (mostly) won it, but to recap the key lessons:

1. **You cannot be prolific without the right mindset**. You are what you think, and you are what you write.
2. **"Doing the work" must be enough for you.** Enough said.
3. **Determine your "why."** Why do you write? Understanding this will keep you going in the hard times.

4. **Eliminate all expectations and stop comparing yourself to other authors**. Seriously. Nothing good comes from comparisonitis. Set goals that are strictly within your control. Sales numbers are not in your control; your daily word count is.

5. **Be attached and unattached to your work... at the same time.** As I said in the first *Be a Writing Machine*: "We want readers to love us. We love the power of throwing our whole soul upon our books, losing ourselves in our stories, and letting the book become representative of who we are. The prolific writer can put all of his or her energy into their books, yet be unattached to them. The less prolific writer cannot avoid attachment, and therefore cannot avoid misery. Be, therefore, a prolific writer. Be unattached...It means to do the work that matters, and to do that work with all of your soul...If it doesn't bring you the money, fame, or readers you wanted, that's okay. If you wake up the next morning and realize that a book is the wrong book and you should be writing another book, you should start working on the other book without expending any sadness for what you've already written. Easy to say, hard to do." Heed those words.

6. **Be spirited about the writing process, not your story.** Be passionate about the process of writing, but beware of getting mired in the weeds of quality. Only readers can decide on quality. To quote legendary football coach Arthur L. Williams, "All you can do is all you can do and all you can do is enough."

If you internalize these lessons, you will most certainly win the war against yourself. Self-doubt will still be present in your life, but you will know how to manage it better than most.

What comes next: higher levels of understanding, self-awareness, and productivity. If you read anything in this section that frightens you or evokes a visceral reaction, ask yourself why. It may not be that the advice is bad—it may be your self-doubt talking.

If you adopt even just a few of the additional ideas in this section, your productivity will zoom light-years ahead.

The Importance of Having Fun

There are few hard and fast rules in the writing world, but I truly believe this one: if you're not having fun with your writing, then you're not doing it right. Dean Wesley Smith always gives this advice, and the more I write, the more I agree.

You probably wanted to become a writer because you enjoy telling stories. You love getting lost in worlds and words. That's what makes writing fun, especially when you work at a soul-sucking job where "fun" isn't in the dictionary.

Therefore, writing is an escape.

If your escape isn't fun, then you will eventually stop doing it. After all, if you work a crappy job, why would you want to escape to another crappy job?

Yet, many gurus frequently teach the virtues of writing to market and writing to trend. These gurus teach a harmful lesson: if you want to make money from your work and achieve your dream, then you must make yourself beholden to what readers want. This means writing a story that you may not enjoy. Even worse, these gurus often vanish into the night. I've seen many of them come and go.

This is damaging for many reasons. While it's true that readers do have expectations, it is much easier to satisfy them than you think. You also don't have to sacrifice your art to do it.

Take this book, for example. You picked up this book because you want to learn how to be a more efficient writer.

Here's what you want:

1. Clear and concise advice.
2. Actionable tips.
3. No hard sells and no preaching.

Did I get that right? If so, as long as I deliver on those expectations, I can get away with a lot, and I have many tools at my disposal to ensure that you find this book helpful.

For fiction, reader expectations are a little more complicated, but not hard:

1. **Your cover, book description, and story should match the book's genre**. If your book is a romance, then there better be a happily ever after. If your book is science fiction, there better be technology. If your book is fantasy, there better be magic. You get the picture.

2. **Your cover, book description, and story should match your book's *subgenre***. Taking our examples further, your sweet romance shouldn't have any sex scenes, your science fiction space opera should be set in space across multiple planets, and your urban fantasy should take place in a city.

3. **If your book is a mash-up of genres, readers still need to know the "main" genre**. If your story is 70 percent space opera and 30 percent post-apocalyptic, then call it a space opera with post-apocalyptic tones. Call it a post-apocalyptic story set in space if it's the other way around.

4. **Your story should contain as many high-level tropes for the subgenre as possible**. Your sweet romance might have a friends-to-lovers story, a slow, simmering romance, and characters with traditional values. Your space opera might have a military main character, a race of evil aliens, and a dark, gloomy mood. Your urban fantasy might have lots of magic and a seedy underbelly with many types of paranormal characters. How many high-level tropes should your story have? It shouldn't be zero, but the more you have, the better.

Note that the guidelines above pertain mostly to the story's structure. They do not dictate what your story should be about. That freedom belongs to you. As it should.

The most important thing you can do is set clear expectations for readers. If you confuse them in any way, you will hurt your sales. But suppose you set clear expectations and link your book to other similar books. In that case, you will find that readers will be very forgiving of stories that veer off the beaten path if you write them well. In fact, readers can and do reward unique and original stories all the time. When you look at these stories, it's often because the author adhered to the high-level tropes but did something innovative with the lower-level ones.

As I said, it is surprisingly easy to meet reader expectations without those expectations dictating your creative approach. You just have to have the courage to write the story in your heart and understand the genres you are working in so you can set expectations accordingly.

Why is this important? Because if you don't keep your writing fun, you will burn out.

Writer's Block vs. Burnout

. . .

Let's talk about the difference between writer's block and burnout.

With writer's block, you can't figure out what to write *for a short period*. I define "short" as a few minutes, hours, days, weeks, or, in severe cases, months.

With burnout, you cannot bring yourself to write for many months or years. You cannot physically or emotionally bring yourself to the writing desk. It is an existential crisis frequently accompanied by mental health issues.

When you write to market and write to trend, your chances of burnout increase significantly.

I knew a fellow self-published author who was so successful that they became a household name in their genre. They sold six figures' worth of books each year, got invited on all the major self-publishing podcasts, and had more money than they knew what to do with. I had dinner with this person and was amazed at their success. Several months later, this author stopped writing and dropped out of existence. Several years after that, the author emailed their newsletter with a long apology about why they had disappeared. The author explained that they had been writing books they didn't believe in and couldn't do it anymore. They wanted to write other stories but couldn't find the joy anymore. Eventually, the author found their way, but in the meantime, their sales dried up and readers forgot about them.

Take that as a cautionary tale for what can happen if you face burnout. It seldom ends well. I've seen a variation on this theme happen to dozens of authors.

If you followed all the advice in this book and became insanely prolific and successful, will it have been worth it if you jeopardized your physical and mental health? Will it have been worth it if you woke up one morning and couldn't find the joy?

For me, the answer is no. I don't care how much money I *could* make; it's just not worth writing stories I don't care about.

You can learn to be a writing machine, but it's not worth it if the machine falls apart. That's why you need to keep the machine in working order. To torture this analogy even further, having fun with your writing keeps the gears lubricated. It also serves as a warranty against burnout.

That's why I cultivate a fun mentality when I write. It keeps me healthy, creative, and well out of burnout's grasp.

Most importantly, keeping writing fun becomes a long-term business advantage. While others are burning out, I'm still having fun with my writing and producing new books.

More fun = more books. More books = more readers. More readers = more income. More income = more freedom. More freedom = more fun. That's a cycle worth believing in!

If you want to avoid burnout in your writing life, follow these steps:

- **Pick the right projects for the right reasons**. When you must decide which book to write, pick the book that makes you jump out of bed in the morning. If you have two projects that you are equally passionate about, pick the project you think will teach you the most lessons. That's the best tiebreaker. (Then, write the other one when you finish that project!)
- **Don't ask for feedback**. We writers want to be loved. We have a natural inclination to ask readers and other writers what they think about our writing. However, you must learn to stand on your own two feet and let your writing speak for itself regardless of what other people think. When you ask for feedback, other people will automatically assume something is wrong with the work. It's a simple law of psychology. An exception to this rule is when feedback is given by an editor, but only when you agree. You can also use alpha and beta readers in a

controlled fashion (which I cover in my book *The Self-Publishing Advice Compendium*). But in general, feedback will introduce negativity into your writing space, and that will only hurt you in the long term.

- **Project confidence.** Writing is like dating…when you meet a potential partner, you can tell if they're comfortable in their own skin or if they're insecure. When you are comfortable with your writing abilities, you will attract people. When you're not, you will repel them. Readers can sense your confidence through your cover, book description, and story itself. In other words, readers will be more likely to have fun when you're having fun as a writer.

- **Be true to yourself, and the money will follow.** I put my heart and soul into every book I write, but I never place any expectations on a book to earn income. When I create a book, the most important thing is that I created it. Against all odds, I persevered and did something that 99 percent of people in the world will never do. I was courageous enough to put that book into the world even if readers don't like it. If even one stranger buys it, that's *amazing*. Could I have higher expectations for my work? Should I? Sure. But the funny thing is that I am successful beyond my wildest dreams, and I believe part of the reason is that I don't place expectations on my work. That gives me complete freedom to write what I want, when I want, with a community of people who want to hear what I have to say because I stayed true to myself.

Trust me when I say that you don't want to burn out. Over the past decade, I have consistently published at least 10 books per year without suffering even an ounce of burnout. I'm exactly the type of writer who should be forever burned out, yet I am always enthusiastic and invigorated with each new book.

People ask me if I have ever burned out; the honest and quick answer is no. How *can* I burn out if I love what I'm writing? It's not possible.

You too should find ways to ensure that burnout is never a dangerous force in your writing life.

Writing Quotas—Yes or No?

In the first *Be a Writing Machine,* I wrote about the power of a daily writing quota. I want to explore that further, because I've learned a lot about writing with one.

Should you write every day?

We can agree that yes, you *should* write every day...but *can* you? That's the challenge.

None of us write in a vacuum. Most of us don't have the privilege of writing from sunrise to sunset. We have families, jobs, other hobbies, and other responsibilities that we must balance with our writing. So, while we *should* write every day, most of us probably can't. There's nothing wrong with that.

For several years, I was lucky if I could find *any* time to write during the day. I wrote when I could, and because I mastered dictation and writing on my phone, I was able to maintain a prolific output.

But I did not have a daily writing quota for the first seven years of my writing career. You may not be able to accomplish a quota either, and that's okay.

However, I have changed my mind about daily writing quotas over the years. While they may not be doable for everyone, there is no doubt that instituting a quota (and sticking to it) will explode your word count in short order.

After I graduated from law school, I suddenly found myself with more time to write, so I decided to ratchet up my discipline and spend all that extra time writing. I instituted a writing quota of 2,000 words per day Monday through Saturday and 1,000 words on Sunday. That meant I needed to write 13,000 words per week, 52,000 words per month, or 672,000 words per year. I slowly increased my quota over time.

Did I hit my quota most days? You bet I did. Did I get upset if I didn't? No, because the law of averages worked in my favor. Some days I was over, some days I was under. It all evened out in the end because I kept writing.

As my productivity has improved, I have focused on achieving what prolific writer Dean Wesley Smith calls "Pulp Speed." Pulp Speed refers to a range of speeds achieved by classic pulp writers. You cannot call yourself a pulp writer unless you write *at least* one million words per year. Many pulp writers wrote many times more than that. Pulp Speed is not easy to achieve unless you have reached the upper echelons of productivity.

If you want to write one million words per year, you have to write approximately 2,750 words every day without fail. If you miss even one day, then you won't achieve the goal. The math gets even more difficult if you only write five days per week. It gets downright brutal if you start missing days.

I believe one million words per year is a wonderful goal to aspire to, even if you never achieve it. Writing even a quarter of that number will make you very prolific in a few years (250,000 / 50,000 = 5 novels per year, and 5 novels in 5 years is 25 novels).

The Mechanics of a Quota

. . .

(Fair warning that there are quite a few numbers in this chapter. I promise that the math is simple, but don't be afraid to read this a few times if you need to.)

If you decide to institute a quota, keep the following best practices in mind.

#1: To start, select a word count that is below what you can currently achieve. Otherwise, you'll become discouraged. If you normally write 1,000 words per day, aim for 800.

#2: Increase your quota gradually until you reach a breaking point. I'm keeping the example above: hit your 800-word quota until you are comfortable and can achieve it for as long as possible. Then, bump it up to 900 words. Do 900 words for a while, then shoot for 1,000. Keep increasing your word count gradually until you start failing regularly. Then, back off that number by 10 percent. That's your optimum writing speed.

#3: Track your progress. Many writing apps can track how many words you write each day, and this is a great way to map your progress. However, no writing app I know of will track your word counts *across all your projects*. For example, if you write a short story and then switch to a novel, you probably store both manuscripts in separate files, so you'll have to add two numbers together to get your daily word count. Your app probably won't track your master word count for the year either. Therefore, I recommend building an external tracker in Microsoft Excel or Google Sheets. You don't need to build anything complicated—just a tool that will help you see your word counts every day over time.

#4: Think in terms of "surpluses" and "deficits." If you have a 1,000-word quota and you write 800 words, then you have a 200-word deficit for the day because you are short. If you write 1,200 words, then you have a 200-word surplus because you're ahead.

#5: Balance your surpluses and your deficits. Let's

take the previous example further. If your quota is 1,000 words per day, that means you need to write 7,000 words per week (1,000 x 7).

Let's say that you write 1,200 words on Sunday. You have a surplus of 200 words. This means that you only have 5,800 words left to write for the week (instead of 6,000). But, let's say that you only write 800 words on Monday (the next day). You eat into your surplus, so, while you only wrote 800 words, you had a 200-word surplus, so you're actually still on track to win the week. Every day will be different; some days you'll end with a great surplus, or you'll end with a major deficit. Sometimes this will happen back to back. This is why it's helpful to understand your weekly, monthly, and annual word count quota. More on this in a minute.

#6: Don't discount weekly, monthly, and yearly quotas. It's easy to focus only on your daily word counts, but when you do that, you lose perspective. Seeing your weekly, monthly, and annual quota will keep you accountable. It allows you to zoom out and take a long-term view of your writing. The daily number only exists to help you understand what you need to be doing to support your long-term goals.

#7: ABAS (Always Be Adding Surplus). Whenever you can, try to operate on a surplus. If you're supposed to write 1,000 words and you hit your quota early, keep writing until it's time to stop. Even if you end your writing session with a 100-word surplus, that will help you for the rest of the week in case life happens.

#8: Use your surplus strategically. When life happens, you can "use" your surplus to skip out on words if needed. If you get sick, use your surplus. If you're going on vacation and want to enjoy it without worrying about words, build up your surplus before you go. This is why you should always add surplus whenever possible because life *will* strike. But honestly, don't use your surplus unless you have to.

#9: Consider a range if the above practices are too

intimidating. Maybe the thought of a single arbitrary number scares you. If so, aim for a range of words every day. Your quota would instead be a range. For example, maybe you aim to write between 800 and 1,000 words every day. 800 is your minimum and 1,000 is your maximum. If you write 800 words, that's a win for the day. If you write greater than 1,000, it's a flawless victory.

This is just another way of thinking about this. You can work your way up to a quota in the long run.

Thinking Long-Term

Most writers think about word counts at the daily level, but if you want to reach new levels of productivity, you should think about word counts at the annual and decade levels.

I know it seems weird. Predicting the future is not easy. You could get hit by a bus tomorrow, but chances are, you won't. If you write 1,000 words today and stay consistent over the next year, you will write 365,000 words.

If you take the math further, you will write 3.65 million words in 10 years. If you write 50,000-word novels, that's 73 novels. That is one fantastic number, and a hell of a library for readers to get lost in.

Most people have no idea what they will be doing 10 minutes from now…10 years from now? Good God.

If you cultivate long-term strategic thinking, you will gain an advantage because while other people focus on a single day, you will focus much further into the future. Doing so will help you regulate your productivity.

Let's say you plan on writing one million words per year, but you fall behind by a week. If you want to meet your goal, then you will need to find time to catch up.

But you *don't have to* catch up if you have a surplus. Let's say you have a surplus of 10,000 words for the year. You're ahead of your plan and exceeding your writing quota each day. You have a family vacation and are worried about taking two days off. Because of your surplus, you can take time off and *still* be ahead of your plan!

That's the advantage of knowing your numbers. Knowledge is power. You will be able to make decisions that will bear better and sweeter long-term fruit than if you stayed focused on just your daily word counts.

Daily word counts are deceptive because you don't have any perspective when you look at one day's worth of numbers. Honestly, you don't have perspective at all until you look at your projected *annual* count. Only then will you know how you're truly doing for the year.

Remember: build a surplus early in the year and keep growing it whenever you can!

Back to Quotas

For now, consider the power of a quota if you can. It will make a gigantic difference in your productivity. When you have a goal to shoot for, you will be more enthusiastic about pursuing it. It will also hold you accountable.

If you're not in a place to execute a writing quota, that's okay too. Do the best you can with the time you have.

Remember the Law of Averages

I have mentioned million-word word counts several times over the last few chapters. If that made you nervous, don't worry. I will dispel some myths in this chapter.

We've already discussed the power of quotas. For example, I said that you need to write 2,750 words per day to achieve one million words per year. Does this mean that you have to write 2,750 words every single day?

No. Not even the most disciplined writers will be able to sustain the same word count every day. After all, you're going to get sick, your family is going to get sick, personal circumstances will intervene in your life, and there will be countless other factors that could result in word count days that are under your quota, or worse—zero.

This is perfectly normal and something you should plan for.

Here's how: remember the law of averages.

When you calculate an average, some words within your range will be higher and some will be lower. If you think about your writing productivity as a bell curve, it's a safe bet to assume that 20 percent of your word counts will be significantly higher or lower than the average. For the sake of easy examples, we could say that 10 percent of your days will be significantly higher than your average—these are the days when you are crushing it. An additional 10 percent of your days will be significantly lower than your average. These are the days when you barely write anything at all.

The remaining 80 percent will consist of numbers near your average. Therefore, you shouldn't worry so much about your high or low days. **The majority of your writing career will be built on your average.**

Understanding this is critical because it takes the sting out of the bad days. My experience has been that the very high and very low days cancel each other out, so I don't pay much attention to them. Sure, there's nothing better than a day where I write significantly more than my average, but the reverse is also true: there's nothing worse than taking a zero-word count day!

Therefore, don't get caught up in the highs and lows. That way lies an emotional roller coaster that will only harm your long-term productivity. On most days, aim to be as close to your average as possible, slightly better if you can.

This advice is also rooted in science. In her book *Dopamine Nation*, Dr. Anna Lembke, an addiction specialist at the Stanford University School of Medicine, writes about the concept of homeostasis. In homeostasis, your body seeks to remain at the same body temperature. This is the condition of optimal functioning for your organs. No matter what you do, the body always seeks homeostasis.

According to Dr. Lembke, the brain is no different. Lembke describes brain homeostasis like a scale with pleasure on one side and pain on the other. Whenever we engage in something that tips the scale in pleasure's favor, little gremlins jump on the pain side, bringing the scale back to balance. This results in pain, which is particularly awful for addiction patients.

By focusing on maintaining balance in your life, you can

live a better life because the gremlins won't bother you as much. I believe this is true with writing too.

Humans love pleasure, but too much pleasure causes pain.

Writers love big word count days, but if you hit too high, your writer brain will crash, resulting in low word count days.

I have had many crazy-high word count days, followed by crazy-low word count days. For example, if I write more than 10,000 words per day (considered to be one of the holy grails of productivity), then I can reasonably expect a low day to be right around the corner. It happens like clockwork. Instead, if I focus on maintaining my average, then my streak will last much longer. I consider this one of the oddest quirks of productivity. It's almost as if the universe tries to put a limit on you.

The best way to avoid this problem is to aim for your average every day. You'll have to look at your own productivity patterns and figure out how to solve the homeostasis problem for yourself, but just be aware that it exists.

Learn to Love Little Word Counts

If you're ever feeling discouraged about your lack of progress toward your word count, I want you to remember this chapter.

If you are facing a zero-word count day and only have a few minutes to write, you should write, even if it results in an extremely low word count for the day.

If you have five minutes before bed and can only write 50 words, write those 50 words.

Here's what most people will do: they will look at those five minutes and decide that it's not worth firing up the computer, loading their manuscript, trying to remember where they left off, and writing. They will gladly take a zero-word count for the day.

Here's what happens when you decide to do the opposite:

- The 50 words you thought you'd write magically expands to 200 or 300 words.
- You don't write for five minutes; your session time magically expands too.
- You maintain momentum that you otherwise would have lost.

- You'll feel great about making progress, which means you will be more likely to have a good writing day the next day.
- Over a year, the numbers magically add up in ways you can't imagine.
- Over a decade, all those little micro word counts become a mighty contributor to your portfolio.

You will reap the benefits when you choose to write micro word counts. You'll be so glad that you did. The hard part is doing it.

The Power of Streaks

A streak is a pattern that persists indefinitely until it is broken. Generally, the longer a streak lasts, the more powerful it is. If we think about our writing habit as a streak, then it possesses a new power.

Streaks are wonderful because of the concept of momentum. It's much harder to get a boulder rolling if it is at rest. But if the boulder is already moving, it's much easier. This is what we call momentum. The more momentum you have, the more effective you will be.

It takes time to build momentum. It doesn't happen overnight. In our case, it doesn't happen in a day or even a week. You build momentum through daily discipline and writing regardless of how you feel. It's not easy.

Goals motivate me, so I love thinking about streaks. Once I start a streak, I do everything in my power to avoid breaking it. When I break a streak, I know it will take me several days to get back into the rhythm I was in before.

Do what you can to keep streaks going. The best way is to record them. This could mean marking off a calendar every day you write (or using a streak feature in your favorite writing app). Or, you could keep track of your streak on your blog or in a diary. However, you do it, keep it visible. The more you can remind yourself of the streak's existence, the more likely you will be to keep it going.

Momentum is critical.

Managing Family and Work

How do you manage writing and all your other responsibilities?

In the first *Be a Writing Machine*, I talked about the concept of work-life harmony, which I believe is a better way to think about juggling all the responsibilities. I've learned the power of work-life harmony on deeper levels.

People talk all the time about work-life balance, but I don't like that term. I prefer "work-life harmony" instead. Balance implies two sides, but your life isn't two-sided. It's multi-faceted.

"Harmony" is a better way to think about this because it encourages you to live a life where all of your passions and responsibilities align. When you have work-life harmony, then work, life, family, and writing blend together into a harmonious song. Whenever they don't, there's dissonance.

Therefore, seek harmony in all areas of your life.

Family

Every family is different.

I am married to a wonderful wife, with an eight-year-old daughter at the time of this writing. I also have a dog, a rabbit, and a turtle. Your family makeup will almost certainly be different from mine, but there are some general guidelines you can follow.

First, family is more important than writing. Unless you are estranged from your family and live alone, nothing is more important than your relationship with your spouse, children, aging parents, and others who live in the home with you. This is critical.

It is important to be on the same page as your family members. If you're going to spend more time writing, then discuss your goals with them and get their support.

Some ideas to help you with the conversation:

1. Always be present at major events, such as sports games, recitals, and other events that are important to your family members. Your writing time should never come at the expense of supporting them.
2. For every minute of extra time you claim for writing that takes away from family time, give that same time to your spouse. For example, if I have a speaking engagement that takes up my Saturday afternoon, my wife will usually schedule some time for herself or with friends immediately after the event is over. This way, she gets some time to herself.
3. Balancing the writing life is like a love language. If you have a supportive spouse, you should also be supportive of them too. That's a basic fundamental of marriage.

It gets complicated when you and your spouse are not on the same page. If your spouse harbors resentment about your writing, then writing more is only going to increase that resentment. This is why it is critical to have a conversation about your goals sooner than later. There's no point in being insanely productive at the cost of your family.

One of the reasons I am so prolific is that my wife is incredibly supportive. But if you were to talk to her, she would also tell you that I am incredibly supportive of her and her hobbies too.

Why am I even talking about this? A few words of caution.

I hate to tell you this, but no matter what you do, your daily word count will never be enough. When you become a writing machine, you become a figurative machine. If you're like me, there is always another book, story, or world to get lost in. If you're *especially* like me, then you can't get to the next book fast enough!

You will *always* want to feed the beast. You will always want to push your word counts a little faster and a little farther. It can be easy to lose perspective once you adopt this mindset.

I hope this chapter will help you stay anchored in what is truly important.

Work

Do you enjoy your job?

I'm not Nostradamus, but I can predict that when it comes to feelings about your job, you fall into one of three categories:

- You love your job.
- You have ambivalent feelings about your job.
- You hate your job.

Your answer to the question will vary depending on the day!

Your job satisfaction has a much greater impact on your writing productivity than you realize.

If you hate your job, you will be more stressed out. The more stressed out you are, the less likely you are to write.

Stress is subconscious. Even if you don't feel stressed per se, it will manifest itself in unusual ways. One of these ways is writer's block. You'll never think, "I'm stressed at work, so I have writer's block," but it will be true.

I used to work as a manager. The job itself wasn't too bad, but the work environment was awful. I was overworked, under-paid, and always expected to do more, more, more. Yet I kept saying, "I'm not stressed."

When I accepted a new job that was much less stressful, I finally realized how stressed out I really was. With the new job, the words came easier. I was able to concentrate better. I was physically and mentally healthier too.

We would all love to quit our jobs and write full-time. If you're like most writers, though, then you probably can't quit your day job yet. If that's true, then you should at least spend some time thinking about your happiness.

Nothing causes dissonance in your life like a job you hate. If you want to be a writer, but your job is preventing you from doing that, maybe consider finding a different job. I know this is easier said than done, but a job is a job. How badly do you want to be a writer? If your job prevents you from even spending a modest amount of time writing each week, one day you'll wake up and realize how much time you've wasted.

I frequently receive emails from authors in their sixties and seventies who tell me that they wish that they had followed their writing dreams sooner. Don't let this happen to you. (If that *is* you, then it's not too late! However, the older we get, the more time becomes our enemy.)

So many people bitch about their jobs but never do anything about it. Over the last decade, one of my secrets to productivity is that, more often than not, I've chosen jobs that allow me work-life harmony. The moment that stopped, I found another job. This has allowed me to publish high numbers of books year after year while also being a high-performer at work. My writing and my work feed off each other.

Are there times when I'm inundated with work and have to put in overtime? Sure, all the time. Every job has busy seasons. But in the end, I still come out ahead. Most days, I log off at the end of my shift. That's the key.

When you like your job, you'll be in a better position to write more. It means you can wake up every morning and enjoy the time you spend doing the work. (Or at least not hate it!) When you're done working, you can leave work at work and come home with a fresh mind ready for storytelling.

When you like your job, you'll have work-life harmony too. All of this helps your writing tremendously. It helps so much that I can't overstate it, honestly.

Recap: The Master Productivity Formula

Let's combine all of this chapter's mindset tricks to paint a bigger picture.

If you want to be a writing machine:

- kick self-doubt's ass
- have fun
- stop writing sloppy
- institute a writing quota
- hit your quota consistently
- focus on hitting your average
- write even when you only have a few minutes and learn to love the little word counts
- seek work-life harmony in your life

When you beat self-doubt, all things become possible.

When you have fun, you'll write more and you'll write better.

When you stop writing sloppy, you will become more efficient and economical with your writing sessions, resulting in increased productivity over time.

Implementing a daily, weekly, monthly, and annual writing quota gives you something to shoot for (and exceed).

When you hit your quota consistently, you will see results quickly.

When you focus on your average, you will sustain your streaks for longer.

When you write every chance you get, even if it's only in small increments, those little writing sessions contribute to your quota and add up in a big way over time.

When you seek work-life harmony, you will find peace in every area of your life, which will make you more prolific. It will also make your writing better.

Yes, there are a lot of components in the formula, and it's not always easy to hit them, but what would happen if you could?

What if you adjusted your mindset? What do you have to lose? Even if you set goals you can't ultimately hit, you'll likely still have *more words* to show for it.

That's a win-win situation if you ask me, but to bring this back to where we started—to do this, you've got to get a handle on your self-doubt or it will sabotage you. Do that, and new levels of productivity and prolificality await you.

Practical Tools to Crush It
Every Day

Now that we've covered mindset, let's get more practical.

This section will cover mastering your tools and unique ways to improve your word counts.

When you combine the tips in the mindset chapter with the approaches I discuss in this section, you will find that you align your goals with your actions more than you may have in the past, and that will be a beautiful thing.

Mastering Your Tools

In this section, I will cover tools you can use to dramatically increase your daily word count. You don't have to use all the tools in this section, but know that every tool has a perfect time and place.

I recommend experimenting with each of these tools to see which ones suit you best. For the others, just remember that I discussed them because you may need them someday.

Mastering Your Writing App

How is your writing app working out for you?

If your face lit up upon reading my question, that's a great sign. It probably means that you have a writing app that you're comfortable with.

If your face didn't light up, you've got some work to do.

I began my career working in Microsoft Word. Word is a fine writing app, but it has problems.

First, it thinks it's smarter than you. It's the equivalent of the precocious kid in a classroom who thinks they know everything but know very little.

Second, it will fight you to the death if you don't use it correctly. You will waste *hours* of your life fighting with it. (The same goes for Microsoft Word equivalents such as Apple's Pages and LibreOffice.)

Third, Word doesn't offer the best writing experience. Write a novel in it, and you will be scrolling for days. Navigating between chapters isn't pleasant, even if you have them set up correctly with proper headers.

Early in my career, I sometimes had only one hour to write. For every 60 minutes I spent writing in Word, I spent 20 minutes squabbling with the software. That's a third of my writing time. Talk about inefficient...

Apps like Microsoft Word, Pages, and LibreOffice are good writing apps, but they are not designed for writers of fiction or nonfiction. They are generalized writing apps that exist to help writers of all kinds. Students, academics, novelists, recipe writers, marketers, and more depend on these apps' reliability to create their documents. Therefore, the app cannot be all things for all people.

If you're a Microsoft Word person, then great—I don't mean any disrespect. I use Word every day with very good reasons to do so. But you will probably be better served with a writing app specifically for fiction and nonfiction. These specialized writing apps have features that make it easier for you to write your book more efficiently.

Specialized writing apps have features that help you outline, draft, edit, and format your books with little to no effort. Many of them will automatically give you better results than if you used Microsoft Word or one of its equivalents. Most professional authors swear by them, and you will too.

The good news is that there are dozens of specialized writing apps on the market. But with so many writing apps, how do you know which one is best for you? There are many styles to choose from.

I wrote a book called *The Writing App Handbook: How to Choose the Best App for Fiction and Nonfiction Writing*. The book covers the most important things you need to know when choosing a writing app, and it provides a comprehensive overview of the most popular features on the market.

Popular specialized writing app features include:

- a "binder" that lets you jump between your chapters with lightning speed
- dark modes and customizable color themes

- outlining tools such as corkboards, timelines, and mind maps
- advanced search, find, and replace
- typewriter modes
- word count trackers
- comments and tracked changes
- e-book and paperback formatting
- and more

With so many choices on the market, there is no excuse to settle for a writing app that doesn't love you back. It may take some trial and error, but I highly recommend embarking on your pilgrimage to find the perfect writing app for you.

When you have the perfect writing app, it becomes an extension of your fingers. It allows you to write faster and more efficiently. You'll also spend less time fighting with the app because it is designed for what you do every day.

Most writing apps offer free trials so you can test them out for a limited time. Take advantage of that.

Other elements you should consider include:

- whether the writing app is an app you install on your computer or web-based
- whether the app has a mobile version if you want to write on the go
- whether the app offers flat fee pricing or a perpetual subscription
- how many features the writing app has

This is a big decision, so take your time. In addition to writing *The Writing App Handbook*, I also put together a free database of writing apps you can use to compare features and pricing. This is an important decision, so don't settle. Find the best fit.

Once you find the best writing app for you, I recommend that you do the following three things:

1. Invest in a premium course to learn the ins and outs of the writing app as soon as possible (if a course exists). If you want to be prolific, then you must understand the writing app on an expert level.
2. Devote several minutes every day to learning something new about the app. This could be buying a book about it, watching a YouTube video, or just playing around with features. Commit to doing this for at least 100 days. Trust me when I say you will get results quickly.
3. Know exactly where to go or who to contact whenever you run into trouble. This could be a social media community, a forum, or a trusted friend. Getting answers to your problems quickly is critical.

Follow these steps, and you will be dangerous in a few months. When you sit down at the writing desk, you will maximize the amount of time you spend *writing*. You will be more creative because you won't have to worry about the learning curve of the writing app. Some writing apps have brutal learning curves.

Don't underestimate the power of mastering your writing app. It is 100 percent within your control, and one of your first important missions. As you become prolific, your productivity correlates to how comfortable you are with your chosen writing app.

Writing on Your Phone

When I say the words "writing on your phone," people have one of the following three reactions:

1. They love it and want to try it themselves.
2. They're open to hearing more.
3. They shudder at the very thought.

Which category do you fall into?

Even if you shuddered at the thought of writing on your phone, hear me out. This short chapter will explain how mastering this writing method can make a big difference in your productivity.

Many apps allow you to write on your phone. Writing apps on your phone usually offer many of the same features as the desktop version, and they allow you to sync between devices so you always have your most up to date manuscript. Start writing on your computer in the morning, and later, when you're on the go, access your manuscript on your phone.

(As a reminder, you can view my free writing app database to find out which apps have mobile versions at www.authorlevelup.com/writingapps.)

. . .

The Mechanics of Writing on Your Phone

The first question I get is "why"?

The second question I get is "how"?

After all, most people don't put "writing" and "smartphone" in the same sentence.

Why write on your phone?

1. You can write anywhere.
2. You're not tied to a computer to write.
3. Your manuscript is always in your pocket and at your fingertips.

Writing on your phone is not intended to be a *primary* writing method. Think of it as a *supplemental* method to help you add words you wouldn't have otherwise been able to achieve.

Now, let's talk about the "how."

My friend Kevin Tumlinson made a post on Twitter expressing interest in learning how to write on his phone. He asked for accessory recommendations. He assumed that the only way to write on your phone was with a Bluetooth keyboard.

I replied to his post and told him I didn't use a keyboard. I told him I used my thumbs! Kevin's head exploded and he immediately invited me on his podcast to discuss how such a thing was possible. Soon after, I converted him to the dark side…

The truth is that there are *three* ways to write on your phone:

1. With your thumbs.

2. With a Bluetooth keyboard.
3. Through dictation (which we will cover in the next chapter).

Let's discuss the first two methods and their pros and cons.

Writing With Your Thumbs

This is the best way to write on your phone. Open your writing app and start typing with your thumbs like you would type a text message.

This method can be slow, but speed isn't the point. Your goal is to pick up where you left off in your manuscript during sessions of reclaimed time. You might only write fifty or one hundred words during a session, and that's okay. The numbers add up dramatically over time.

Let me give you an example of how the math works:

- Let's say you normally type 2,000 words per day and you write an extra 100 words on your phone every day, giving you 2,100 words per day. That's a 5 percent increase in your daily word count.
- If you normally write 730,000 words in a year, that extra 100 words per day would net you an additional 36,500 words, increasing your annual word count to 766,500. If you write 50,000-word novels, 36,500 represents approximately 73 percent of a novel.
- Put another way, writing just a few words on your phone daily will accumulate into over two-thirds of an extra novel in a year. Over ten years, that would be an extra 7.3 novels!

The pros of this method are that it's easy—just pull out your phone and start typing. Once you get used to the mindset shift of writing on your phone, this method works extremely well because there is almost no friction. Just remember where you left off and start typing.

I have written novels at the doctor's office, in the backseat of Uber cars, on public transit, while standing in the checkout line at the grocery store, and in far more scenarios than I ever thought possible. As I said, the numbers add up dramatically.

Another pro of this method is that it works very well for people with busy lifestyles. If you're not in front of a computer often, this may be the *only* way you can write on some days. This was certainly true for me when I worked a hectic job with frequent travel. Without being able to write on my phone, I would have had to take zero-word count days while on the road, hurting my momentum.

That said, there are some cons to this writing method. The first is that you have to write with your thumbs. That may not be feasible for some people. If you have wrist pain or a history of carpal tunnel syndrome, writing on your phone with your thumbs may be a losing proposition.

Also, writing on your phone may feel unnatural for some. Some people simply cannot associate typing with their thumbs with writing quality words because it reminds them of text messaging. I believe this is a mindset limitation that can easily be overcome with time and practice.

Writing on Your Phone with a Bluetooth Keyboard

There is no doubt that writing on a phone with a Bluetooth keyboard is more ergonomic. It will feel closer to the experience of writing on your computer. For this reason alone, many people prefer to have a keyboard.

Bluetooth keyboards are relatively inexpensive and pair easily with a phone or tablet. They're easy to slip into a backpack, and some come with carrying cases.

You can also type faster on a Bluetooth keyboard than you can with your thumbs, giving you more speed.

However, there are numerous cons. First, you must bring your keyboard with you wherever you go. This is simply not possible when you are on the go or in a hurry. You'll only be able to use this method in areas where you have ample space and the ability to sit down.

The next con is slightly related: you will have to take time to hook up your keyboard whenever you want to use it. This means that you must ensure that it is charged and pairs effortlessly with your device. If you only have a few minutes, the setup time will chip away at your productivity. And, you've got to remember to keep your phone and keyboard sufficiently charged.

That said, Bluetooth keyboards are perfect for afternoons at the coffee shop and writing sessions on your couch.

One of my favorite writing sessions with a Bluetooth keyboard was sitting on my couch while watching my daughter play in the backyard with her friends. I used the Airplay feature on my phone to project the app onto the flatscreen television in my living room. It worked very well, and I wrote 1,000 words to show for it!

Final Words

One limitation worth discussing with writing on your phone is the screen size. This is a turnoff for some people, but phone screen sizes are getting bigger every year. Some phones these days have screens that rival tablets. However, if you have an eyestrain problem, I acknowledge that this method may be more difficult for you.

But if you're willing to try writing on your phone, it's a wonderful supplemental writing method that will contribute greatly to your word counts.

Dictation

I love dictation.

If you want to write faster, spend more time typing. If you want to write blazing fast, then learn dictation.

Dictation is the act of speaking your story. Some dictation styles require you to speak the punctuation; others do not. The common link between them all is that you can simply start talking, which reduces friction. Some people find it easier to speak their stories, especially when they have writer's block.

There are many ways to dictate, and I will cover all of them in this chapter. Not all dictation methods are created equal.

The world's most productive and fastest writers alive today are likely using dictation to achieve their word counts. If you master this writing style, it is not uncommon to improve your daily word count by thousands of words. It's that effective, and nothing comes close to it.

While I believe many writers can benefit from this method, dictation does have a severe learning curve. It's not for everyone. But if it's for YOU, you will be able to write more words than you ever thought possible.

Before we go further, I want to let you know that I wrote a

book called *How to Dictate a Book* that covers dictation in greater detail if this chapter resonates with you.

Phone and Computer Dictation

The easiest way to get started with dictation is to use the dictation feature on your smart phone. Simply tap the microphone button on your keyboard, speak, and watch your voice translated into text in near real time.

The only disadvantage to dictating on your smartphone is the microphone time limit. On iPhones, there is a 60-second cut-off—the microphone stops recording and you have to press it again to continue. That's not helpful if you want to multitask while dictating, but it's perfect if you want to play around with the technology.

You can also get started with dictation on your computer using Google Docs and Microsoft Word. Both have dictation features as well, and they are just as accurate as the software on your phone. However, you will need to ensure that you are as close to your computer's microphone as possible because the distance matters. Also, the microphone on your computer is not likely to be as good as your smart phone's, so your mileage may vary.

Smart phone dictation and computer dictation have improved over the last few years and are stunningly accurate. Best of all, this method is free, so it doesn't cost you anything to try it.

If you've never dictated before, I recommend trying it on your phone and/or computer first, but understand that there are better ways.

On-Screen Dictation

. . .

The most popular dictation method is to use Dragon (by Nuance Software), which is voice-to-text software. Everyone agrees the Dragon is the best speech-to-text software on the market. It has been around for a long time.

There are several versions of Dragon, but I recommend Dragon Professional Individual because it allows for transcription, which we'll cover later. The app is not cheap, but it is well worth the money.

Dragon is only available on Windows operating systems at the time of this writing. The Mac version has been discontinued. This puts Mac users at a disadvantage; the only way to run Dragon is to install a virtual machine such as Parallels so that you can run Windows on your Mac. That's what I do, and it works great.

(Side note: Nuance Software, the creator of Dragon, was purchased by Microsoft in 2021. There are rumors that Dragon will eventually be retired and incorporated into Microsoft Office. If this happens, we may see better cross-platform support in the future.)

To use Dragon, you open an approved writing application (usually Microsoft Word), speak your story, and watch as Dragon converts your words to text in real time. This is called on-screen dictation.

For best results with on-screen dictation, you must use a professional microphone, typically of the podcast variety. Otherwise, your audio quality won't be high enough and you'll get poor results.

Another key feature of Dragon is what I call "Dragonese." In Dragonese, you must speak your punctuation.

For example, let's say I want to say the sentence "'I went to the store,' he said."

If I were to speak this in Dragonese, I would say: open quote I went to the store comma close quote he said period.

This style can feel stilted and artificial because we don't speak our punctuation when we talk naturally. A human listener picks up on punctuation without needing to hear it; a computer cannot, which is why we must speak Dragonese.

Speaking punctuation can slow you down, but it's not so bad if you take the time to get used to it. It's like riding a bike —once you learn how to ride a bike, you never forget. The same is true with speaking punctuation; once things "click," you will always be able to do it, even if you haven't done it for a while. But learning how to speak Dragonese is an adjustment.

On-screen dictation is how many authors get started with Dragon. It's easy to set up and easy to understand. That said, there are downsides.

On-screen dictation requires you to execute several skills at the same time: you must think of what to say, say it, verify that Dragon converted your speech-to-text properly, and edit mistakes. It's a gargantuan task.

Seeing your text generate in real time on the screen is wonderful, but Dragon doesn't always get it right. It frequently mishears proper nouns, for example. Also, if you don't enunciate, it may not hear conjunctions such as "and," "for," or "of." You also may not see that Dragon missed those articles either. They're easy to miss even when you're paying extra attention.

Another downside with on-screen dictation is that even if you speak perfectly, Dragon may still misunderstand you. The software offers verbal commands to help you edit your text with your voice, but they are not always reliable.

My rule of thumb is that your on-screen dictation sessions should give you a 96 percent or better accuracy. If your accuracy is less than that, then you must learn to speak more clearly or troubleshoot issues with the software or your microphone.

On-screen dictation can be quite messy, and you may frequently get the urge to correct your text with your fingers as you type. If your session is going badly, you may stop dictating altogether and revert to typing, defeating the purpose and killing your speed. That's why I call this method hybrid writing —it's often a mixture between speaking and typing.

Believe it or not, on-screen dictation is the *slowest* dictation method. It's a good skill to build, but it often results in sloppy writing that can be discouraging to some people. After all, what's the point if you dictate at the speed of a tortoise?

Dragon Anywhere

Dragon also offers a smartphone application called Dragon Anywhere, which functions much like its computer counterpart, but allows you to dictate on the go. Dragon Anywhere is available with a subscription. It is the best option for Mac users who cannot install Windows on their computers.

I used Dragon Anywhere for about two years and enjoyed it. The accuracy isn't as high as Professional Individual, and it has some oddities, but it's a very good option if you want the power of Dragon but can't run it on your Mac.

Transcription (via Software)

Transcription is the gold standard of dictation. With transcription, you record yourself speaking on a device like your phone or a dedicated voice recorder. Then, you upload the audio to Dragon, and Dragon will convert your audio to text *as if you sat in front of the screen and dictated it.*

You might be wondering why you would need to transcribe your text. As I mentioned in the previous section, on-screen dictation requires you to do several things at the same time: think, speak, verify, and edit. Transcription removes the verify and edit steps. Therefore, you only have to worry about thinking and speaking. You then upload the audio to Dragon, which transcribes your text so that you can verify and edit it later. Transcription reduces friction and it enables you to speak your stories much faster.

To transcribe, you must first record high-quality audio. Options include:

- a dedicated voice recorder
- a voice memo app on your smart phone
- a recording app on your computer, such as GarageBand

However you record the audio, you must have a device with a high-quality microphone. This is why many authors recommend dedicated voice recorders. A voice recorder is built to capture the human voice, and it does it extremely well. The microphone on your laptop? Not so much.

The higher-quality microphone you use, the better your results. This doesn't mean that you should go into debt to purchase a high-quality microphone for transcription; it simply means that your device needs to be *good enough*.

What is good enough?

I use a Sony UX 570 voice recorder. It cost me approximately $70. There are many alternatives within this price range.

If you already have a podcasting microphone, that will produce fantastic transcription results too. An entry-level podcasting microphone will give you results that are more than good enough for quality dictation, though you will be tied to your desk for dictation sessions.

The beauty of dictating on a voice recorder or phone is that you can do it anywhere, any time. For example, I dictated this chapter in my car while I was driving to an eye doctor appointment! Others like to dictate while on hikes.

The secret to accurate voice recorder dictation and transcription is to follow what I call the Dictation Pyramid. The pyramid has three sides:

1. distance from mouth to microphone
2. enunciation
3. environment

The first side is the distance from mouth to microphone. The closer the voice recorder is to your mouth, the more accurate your transcriptions will be.

When many people use voice recorders, they hold the recorder to their mouths. This is unwise because the distance from the microphone to your mouth will vary throughout the recording. If you lower your arm even slightly, the quality of the audio will dip, resulting in Dragon potentially mishearing what you said. Therefore, you should aim to keep the microphone at the same distance from your mouth at all times. The best practice is for the microphone to be approximately two inches from your mouth. (You also want to make sure that your audio is not clipping—talking too loudly will also reduce the quality of your dictation.)

I purchased a harmonica neck holder from Amazon. I slip my voice recorder into the holder, then put the holder around my neck. No matter how I move my body, the microphone stays in a fixed position, resulting in more consistent, higher-quality recordings that are easier for Dragon to transcribe.

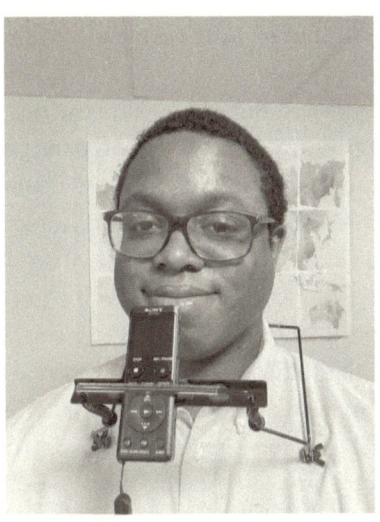

This is a harmonica neck holder with a Sony UX570 inside.

The second side of the Dictation Pyramid is enunciation. You can "train" Dragon to recognize certain words, but you'll find that Dragon goofs the same words consistently. The key is to slow down and speak as clearly as you can. I often speak articles softly, which causes all sorts of problems with transcription. I've learned to slow down and enunciate carefully when I dictate, especially articles. By doing this, I have improved the accuracy of my transcriptions.

The third side of the Dictation Pyramid is the environment. If you dictate in a noisy environment, your accuracy will suffer. If you dictate in a quiet room, you'll get amazing results. The problem is when you are dictating outside or in a room with moderate noise.

The best thing to do is avoid dictating in noisy environments, but sometimes that's not possible. For example, I frequently dictate when I am washing the dishes. You can hear clinking dishes and running water in the recording. In that case, I must speak louder and enunciate even more when the water is running.

Some people like to dictate outside on hikes or long walks, which is relaxing and a great form of exercise. I recommend investing in a lapel microphone with a windscreen designed to minimize outdoor noise. The lapel mic hooks into your voice recorder and you place it on the lapel of your shirt. To keep your hands free, you can slide the voice recorder into your pocket (or a clip-on phone carrier). Engage the "hold" button so you don't accidentally turn off the recorder while walking. It looks better than walking around with a harmonica neck holder, and you'll get good results. I like to route the wires of the lapel mic under my shirt so that passersby don't even know it's there. Sure, I look a little awkward walking around and talking to myself, but hey, that's the price I pay for efficiency!

Dictating in the car also creates a noisy environment. I get great results with a lapel mic in my car.

The lapel mic can go on the lapel of a shirt or blouse. Just keep it as high as possible.

This is a lapel mic with a winter setup. The trick is to keep the microphone as close to your mouth.

If you must carry the voice recorder in your hand, purchase a wrist strap. Most recorders allow you to attach a strap. This way, you won't break the recorder if you accidentally drop it.

I find that my harmonica neck holder gives me a dictation accuracy of around 97 percent; my lapel mic is around 94 percent. There is a difference, but the results are still good overall.

Your technology and your technique matter. By following the laws of the Dictation Pyramid, you will achieve fantastic accuracy with your transcriptions.

Transcription (via a Human Transcriptionist)

Some people don't like Dragon. After all, speaking Dragonese is unnatural and will slow you down.

Another option is to dictate without speaking your punctuation. Then, hire a human transcriptionist to transcribe the audio. The transcriptionist will understand your punctuation and insert the proper marks accordingly. They will also do light editing and formatting.

This method is expensive and time-consuming. Transcriptionists aren't cheap, and you will pay by the minute. It will also take your transcriptionist several days to produce transcripts, which is not ideal because recordings will be "locked up" and you won't have access to what you wrote unless you listen to the recording.

However, you don't have to worry about speaking Dragonese, which means that you can speak much faster. It's a trade-off that you should consider.

When I adopted voice recorder dictation, I tripled my daily word count. If I hired a human transcriptionist and didn't have to speak Dragonese, I bet I could double my word count *again*. Not kidding.

This is simply an alternative to transcription that you should be aware of. If you are ever injured, can't type, or don't want to worry about speaking punctuation, for example, this method could be very useful to you someday. It could also be useful if you are ever under a tight deadline.

Advanced Transcription Methods to Overcome Sloppy Writing

If you follow the dictation methods in this chapter, you will increase your word counts significantly. However, there's one problem: sloppiness.

No matter your dictation method, your dictation sessions will be sloppy. It's just a matter of *how* sloppy. Unless you are willing to develop an additional skill set, there is no way around this.

Yet, you'll recall that I recommended *against* sloppy writing. So why would I recommend dictation at all?

The method I'm about to describe is *extremely* advanced and not for the faint of heart. I will only cover it briefly just so you know that it exists.

My secret involves a little elbow grease and Microsoft Word macros. A macro is a command that performs a series of steps automatically. For example, I can create a macro to automatically apply a certain header style to the first sentence of every chapter in a Word document. This way, I don't have to format each chapter name manually. The macro does this automatically.

I developed special commands that I use when I'm dictating. I hired a programmer to create a Microsoft Word macro that cleans up my text according to the commands. It can do things like delete misspoken sentences and paragraphs, create ordered and unordered lists, apply formatting, and even insert comments. It makes the edits as tracked changes in the document.

This macro is my secret weapon, and it has enabled me to dictate *extremely* clean. I spend very little time cleaning up my text because I can edit it in real time as I speak. This has enabled me to write even more words per day.

As I said, Microsoft Word macros are not for the faint of heart, but if you are willing to learn how to use them, I am confident that you will become a writing machine and one of the most prolific and productive authors in the world.

But as I said, this is extremely advanced and only worth trying if you are more driven than most. You don't have to know any code, but you do have to know how to work with a programmer.

· · ·

Final Words on Dictation

If you'd like to learn more about my dictation methods, read my book *How to Dictate a Book*.

Dictation is amazing. It will help you achieve astronomical word counts, but beware of sloppy writing. If you do it, take your time, speak clearly, and find ways to reduce mistakes.

AI-Assisted Writing

As technology progresses and we move into an era of artificial intelligence, we will see a proliferation of AI-assisted writing apps. These apps allow you to write a small number of words, click a button, and generate high-quality text generated by AI that continues your narrative as if you had written it, usually in increments of a few hundred words.

The app I use at the time of this writing is Sudowrite, but there are many on the market and there will be more in the future.

A few years ago, early versions of these apps produced laughable results. No one's laughing now. At the time of this writing, AI-assisted writing apps are mostly used for copywriting and straightforward nonfiction of an informational nature. In the near future, they will evolve into fiction writing. At some point, they will be able to write entire novels.

These apps can be a great way to boost your daily word count in addition to being a wellspring of new ideas. These apps will frequently recommend narrative paths that you never considered before. Start writing your chapter, click a button, and see where the AI takes you.

In my novel *Year of the Rat (The Chicago Rat Shifter Book 3)*, I experimented with an AI-assisted writing app. I wrote a scene where my main character is at a bus station. I activated the AI to see what it would recommend. The results weren't very good. However, it recommended that my hero encounter a beggar on a bench who asks him for money. *That* was a very interesting idea, and it led to another idea, which helped me write what I thought were the most engaging chapters in the book. So, while the AI recommended that I put a beggar in the story, the words I used were my own. In this sense, the AI served as a co-pilot. I remained in control. This is a wonderful way to think about AI as a writer.

In my experiments with this technology for nonfiction, I have found that the AI recommends different angles of an argument. It does a great job of helping me round out my arguments so I can be more persuasive. I also find that, on average, AI-assisted writing apps help me expand my word counts by about 200 to 400 additional words per writing session.

These apps aren't perfect, though. Sometimes the text reads like enlightened gibberish. Or, the app will recommend paths that don't make sense. These apps will also generate text that is not in your author voice, so if you like the words it recommends, you have to be careful not to just accept them without editing. Otherwise, readers will know when the AI is writing, and you don't want that. If you write a substantial amount of your novel with an AI app, you should also consider disclosing that to readers on your copyright page.

I don't use these apps frequently, but they are great to use when I am sitting at the computer and need some inspiration. They're also great for short-form work like poetry and short stories.

Keep an eye on this technology, because it will continue to evolve rapidly. I predict that, in the near future, it will be ubiquitous and interwoven with the writing apps we know and love. When used correctly and ethically, there's no doubt that these apps can be useful.

Optimizing Your Writing Space

The space you devote to writing deserves a special mention. After all, you're going to be spending a lot of time there.

First, if you can, it helps to have a dedicated writing space. If you live in a tiny apartment, then that could be a desk. If you live in a house, then it could be a room. Either way, you should dedicate a space that exists solely for your writing.

If possible, your writing space should have a door so it's obvious when you're writing. Shut that door when the words are flowing.

Your Desk

I worked for years at an uncomfortable desk, and I have lifelong neck and back pain to show for it. Don't let that happen to you. Your writing desk is perhaps your most important asset, so treat it accordingly.

The desk that caused me neck and back pain? I bought it at a department store sale. If I could travel back in time, you couldn't pay me to purchase it.

Now I have a standing desk. I paid money for a premium standing desk, and it has been one of the best investments of my writing career. Ever. I stand half of every day. Sitting is the new smoking, so it pays to stand.

If you purchase a standing desk, you should also purchase a standing mat. These are usually gel mats that you can stand on to make your standing sessions more comfortable. I received one for free with my standing desk, but you can also purchase them cheaply online.

I also customized my desk to be more suitable for podcasting and speaking engagements—I purchased cheap accessories on Amazon to help me achieve that purpose. The result is a desk that is comfortable and enjoyable to stand at and healthy too! This aids my creativity.

I also purchased a treadmill from a neighbor that I can slide under the desk when I want to walk and write at the same time. I also purchased a recumbent exercise bike with a desk attachment that I can rest my laptop on. There's no excuse for me to write in a sedentary fashion anymore.

Also, I keep my desk relatively uncluttered. I *hate* junk on my desk. Everything has a place and everything is in its place. Sitting down at a clean desk makes it easier to be creative.

Think about it: you want to sit down and write, but your writing space is filled with junk. Therefore, your brain will also be filled with junk. What is on your desk is what is on your mind.

Another element of clutter to consider is your wires and accessories. Nothing is worse than spaghetti all over your desk. Find ways to hide wires and reroute them under your desk. You can purchase wire management kits to help.

Your Chair

. . .

We must also talk about your chair. I also spent years of my life working on uncomfortable chairs that wreaked havoc on my lower back. I highly recommend spending the money on an ergonomic office or gaming chair for your writing. While you will have to spend money, these chairs aren't expensive. I purchased my current ergonomic chair at my local Costco for around $90. (Yes, $90 *could* be considered expensive, but if you have to go to the doctor for chronic back pain because you didn't use the right chair, that's going to cost you a lot more than $90. Keep things in perspective. Once it starts, chronic pain is for life.)

Once, my wife and I went to purchase take-out at a local restaurant. The office next door was getting rid of their furniture due to going out of business. Sitting next to the dumpster was a clean and pristine ergonomic chair that was worth several hundred dollars—free for the taking. You can bet that I loaded that puppy into my SUV faster than you can say pizza. My wife uses that chair every day and swears by it. My point is that you can also find ergonomic chairs in the wild.

Whatever type of chair you buy (or find), you want one with adjustable height and armrests, lumbar support, and, if it suits you—wheels.

If you want to be a writing machine, there's no point in spending more time writing if it's at the expense of your back and neck.

Ergonomic Mouse and Keyboard

Your mouse and keyboard are the tools of your trade. Get them wrong and you'll increase your chances of repetitive stress injuries such as carpal tunnel syndrome. No one wants that.

First, pick the right mouse. Once, I bought a cheap travel

mouse and thought it would work well. It ended up causing cramps in my hand. Make sure your mouse is the proper size. If you must, use a trackball. Consider purchasing a mousepad with a wrist rest.

Second, pick the right keyboard and make sure you've adjusted it correctly. Keeping your keyboard flat is okay, but you may be better off adjusting it so that it meets your fingers at an angle. You may also want to invest in an ergonomic keyboard that has keys strategically placed to minimize wrist pain.

If you don't have wrist pain after long writing sessions, you have the right equipment and are using it correctly. If not, you'll need to make adjustments.

Lighting and Other Miscellaneous Items

Your writing space should be well-lit. Bad lighting is hard on your eyes, and detrimental to your long-term ocular health.

I also worked in a dark room for years, and I don't recommend it. Invest in a lamp or other light source to ensure that you can see the words you're writing. Even if you turn the lights down low, you should still have a lamp on your desk that illuminates the screen.

You probably already have a spare light around your house, so repurpose what you can before spending money. Until just a few years ago, I was still using a lamp I owned in college. It served me well for almost a decade.

If you must spend money, invest in light that will also make your space look more visually appealing. Avoid cheap lamps from big box stores or anything that puts out massive heat. You want a bright, cool light source. No light is completely cool, but you don't want an artificial sun shining on your desk. Not only will that be uncomfortable, but it could also shorten the life of the things on your desk.

Finally, consider ways to make your space more inviting. I like essential oils, so I have a diffuser on my desk that runs during my writing sessions. The fragrances relax me. I also love to listen to music, so I usually have my favorite music playing as I write. I also have LED lighting in my office that I use for mood.

Other ideas to make your space more serene include:

1. Sound machines
2. Candles
3. A new paint job on the walls
4. An area rug on the floor
5. Photos of friends and family

However you decorate your writing space is up to you. As I said, you're going to spend a lot of time there. Make it worthwhile.

More Time Management Secrets

Let's talk about time management. Time management is, quite simply, how you manage your time. We all have the same 24 hours in the day.

If there is anything I have learned over the years, it's that time management is a state of mind. Either you are a natural at it and never have to think about it very much, or you are always struggling to find time to do anything. Time management is either intuitive for you, or it's not.

But here's the secret: it boils down to how badly you want to write. If you really want to become a writer, you will find the time to write. If you really want to be prolific, you will find the time to do so. Honestly, it doesn't matter what I say; only you can decide your destiny.

Where I come in is helping you align your everyday actions with your intentions. That's one of my greatest skills.

Three Ways to Cut a Hole in The Time-Space Continuum

. . .

Let me give you a framework. What you do with this framework is up to you, but I'll give you examples of how I've used this framework in my own life.

At the end of the day, there are only three things you can do with time:

1. Subtract
2. Add
3. Edit

Subtracting Time

When I graduated from college, I had several hobbies. First, I was an English major, so I wrote poetry and short stories. Second, I played video games. I was an avid Japanese RPG gamer. I also wrote game reviews for a major video game review site. Third, I was a musician, and I wrote music, played multiple instruments, and took private lessons.

When I decided to become a writer, my other hobbies frequently got in the way of my writing. If a fun new video game came out, that would wreck my productivity for days; if I came up with an idea for a new song, I would spend hours composing, often well into the night.

When I decided to devote myself to writing, I realized that music and video games were preventing me from being a more successful writer. I decided to stop pursuing those hobbies. I sold all of my video games and instruments to fund the publication of my first book, and I never looked back.

Was it painful? Absolutely. It killed me not to play the latest entries in the *Final Fantasy* series in particular, but a writer's gotta do what a writer's gotta do.

I applied this mindset to every area of my life, subtracting anything that did not serve my goal of becoming a writer. To twist the cliché, I put my time where my mouth was. You can judge my results for yourself.

I'm not saying you should give up all of your hobbies. If there is a non-writing activity that brings you joy that you can't bear to give up, that's fine, but remember that life is finite. You will go much further much faster if all your dogs are pulling in the same direction. The better your focus, the better your results.

Adding Time

The opposite of subtracting time is adding time. This means finding extra time in the day to write.

I am a morning person. I love waking up before dawn and working on my books. My wife and daughter are not morning people. It takes them a long time to get out of bed in the morning. Therefore, I add time to my day by waking up early and devoting the first hours to writing. Sure, I have to sacrifice some sleep, but I just go to bed earlier. Problem solved.

If you're a night owl, find time to write at the end of your night.

The key is to find time at the beginning or end of your day and anchor your time around it. Even if you do this a couple of times a week, you will notice the difference, and you will feel great. It's like starting a new workout routine at the gym—the first few sessions are painful, but you will see results quickly. And once you see those results, you won't want to stop pumping those weights—I mean, writing those words...

This method is arguably harder than subtracting time

because it requires discipline. If you love your sleep, then you will have to sacrifice some of your dream time to pursue your real dream. Naturally, I don't condone harming your health to be a writer, but finding time in the morning or late at night is something I want you to think about. I bet you can do it safely if you develop discipline.

Editing Time

This method is the most transformative time management tip. Master this, and people will think you are a superhuman.

What do I mean by "editing" time?

Let me give you many examples.

I was at the doctor's office and the doctor was running late. I pulled out my phone, opened my writing app, and made progress on one of my chapters.

What most people would have done: waste time on their phones.

I was in New York City for a writing conference and took an Uber to and from my hotel. In true New York fashion, the drivers weren't very talkative, and I had 45 minutes to kill. I pulled out my phone and made progress on my novel.

What most people would have done: stared out the window, daydreamed, wasted time on their phones, or tried to have a conversation with a driver who wasn't interested.

I was on a three-hour flight. I pulled out my phone and made progress on my novel.

What most people would have done: anything but that, especially if the plane had an infotainment system with free movies and television shows.

I had to deliver some furniture to my in-laws who live 45 minutes away. I was in the car by myself. I brought my voice recorder with a lapel mic, hooked the mic on my shirt, put the voice recorder in my cupholder, and dictated sections from my novel on the road.

Most people would have listened to the radio, called a long-time friend, or just drove.

I hope you get it by now. It's unwieldy to take your laptop or tablet everywhere you go to write your books, but being able to write books on your phone is a godsend. I know this method is not for everyone, and I know some people simply cannot do this for health reasons. However, this has been a game changer for me, and it is how I "edit" my time. While other people are wasting time on their phones, I am being productive. Yes, I watch just as much YouTube as the next person, but I only do it when I achieve my word count. That takes discipline and a willingness to retrain your brain to always be looking for writing time.

Dictation is also a major way I edit my time.

I walk my dog several times per day. I bring my voice recorder and lapel mic and dictate my novel while taking a neighborhood stroll. Each walk usually results in at least 500 words. Three walks per day means 1,500 extra words per day *without even sitting down at my computer.* Plus, my dog loves it!

When I type, I can normally write about 2,000 words per hour if I'm inspired. Usually, it's less than that. When I dictate, I can speak between 3,000 and 4,000 words per hour on average. If I spend the same time writing but dictate instead, I have just optimized my time to get in double the number of words. That's another way to edit time.

Editing time is great, but I want to leave you with a few words of caution: **if you want to write on your phone or dictate while out in public, always maintain situational awareness**. Don't write when it's not safe to do so. I only write on the go if I can do it safely.

For example, I dictate in my neighborhood while on walks because I know my neighbors and my neighbors know me. I also know the dogs, cats, squirrels, and where common trouble spots are for my dog (she's a frustrated greeter and barks like mad at other dogs). When needed, I stop dictating and focus on my dog.

I only dictate while driving on roads I am familiar with. I live in a small city, so that makes it easy. I never dictate in school zones or residential areas with lots of children.

Some critics of my methods have said that they would find it exhausting to be thinking about writing all the time. However, it's not exhausting for me because I pick the right projects for the right reasons. I am always excited to get back into the land of my story. This isn't a job for me. It's a passion. If it was a job, then yes, it would be exhausting.

But if you're willing to find ways to edit your time, I am confident that you will like the results.

Think about how you spend your time on your phone: do you waste it on Facebook or trivial internet searches? Do you spend more time in your email app than you should? Do you have text message conversations that go nowhere? Do you watch videos endlessly, or play games that ultimately don't matter? If the answer to any of those questions is yes, then what do you have to lose by diverting just *some* of that time to the activity that you are truly passionate about?

For me, it's a no-brainer. Like I said, align your activities with your intentions.

Writing Even Smarter

Let's talk about the mechanics of your writing day. In other words, what do you do with your time once you maximize your time and master the writing methods that work best for you?

This chapter will help you create the perfect writing session, every time.

How You Start is How You End

Know the golden rule of productivity: how you start is how you will finish.

If you usually write in the morning but wake up late, scramble out of bed, and stumble through your day, your word count will suffer. Conversely, if you wake up on time, eat breakfast, and perform your other daily rituals in addition to writing, you will have a better day.

I have tracked my word counts for the last several years, and I can safely say that any day where I don't write in the morning has the potential to be a zero-word day. If I start the day with a healthy word count, I am more likely to hit my quota or even have a surplus for the day. If I don't, I have to work extra hard to meet my goals.

Case in point: the day I wrote this very chapter, I was pulled into work unexpectedly for an important meeting, which meant that I had to give up my writing time in the morning. Because of the events of the day, I didn't start dictating until 4:30 p.m. I had to spend the entire evening catching up. I was fortunate to hit my quota for that day, but it could have just as easily been a zero-word count day.

Because I know this golden rule, I know when to compensate and reorganize my day accordingly.

If you're a night owl, then the golden rule is the opposite: how you end your day will determine how strong your word count is. For example, if you don't normally start writing until 10 p.m., make sure you start writing at 10 p.m. Don't put it off. Every minute that passes increases your chances exponentially of having a zero-word count day (or missing your quota, if you have one). Therefore, your main goal should be to organize your day so that you can start writing on schedule as many days as possible. Do that, and you will meet your goals.

If you're a scattered writer without a set time during the day, your situation is much more perilous. I can relate because my schedule is quite hectic as well. You will have to find the rhythm that works best for you and know when the ideal writing times are. When they happen, don't delay. Start writing.

The trick with a schedule like this is to be diligent and disciplined. There's no time for dawdling. Sit down at the computer or pull out your phone if a moment arises. No exceptions, no bullshit. Just do it. It's easier said than done, but remember—your actions should align with your goals. If you want to be a prolific writer and you're not getting those words in when the time is right, you are undermining your goals.

Don't Start Your Day with Editing

There's nothing wrong with editing during your writing sessions, but remember what I said about editing: when you're revising, you're not generating new words.

New words must be your priority.

Here's the first problem with editing: you're more likely to keep editing when you edit. It's harder to shift into being creative. When you start with editing, you're working against your goals.

Here's the second problem with editing: you enter a critical state of mind when you edit. Dean Wesley Smith calls this the critical voice. Your critical voice points out problems with your work, and its goal is to protect you. Sometimes that protection comes in the form of making you want to quit or feel bad about the work. Your critical voice's goal is to sabotage your writing.

The opposite of the critical voice is the creative voice. The creative voice is your muse. This is where your stories come from. Dean Wesley Smith often refers to the creative voice as a two-year-old child and the critical voice as a parent. A child is innocent and doesn't know the dangers of the world; the parent is jaded and always wants to protect the child. In our case, when the critical voice tries to "protect" us, it comes in the form of persuading us to quit.

Telltale signs of the critical voice include:

- feeling inadequate
- feeling incompetent
- feeling inferior
- feeling like your work is crappy (when you were excited about it days, hours, or minutes earlier)
- thoughts of quitting
- thoughts of rewriting

Often, the critical voice makes criticisms of your work with no factual basis to do so. Just because the critical voice says your work is crap, that may not be true. You could simply be having a bad day.

Beware of your emotions. They will play games with your writing.

For example, one day, I woke up in an odd mood. I checked my work email and received a message from my boss that put me in a bad mood. I hadn't even gotten out of bed yet. The entire day, everything sucked. Work sucked, my writing sucked, and everything in my personal life went wrong. I was late getting my daughter to school. I hit a traffic jam. I logged in to work late. Projects blew up, customers sent angry emails, and more. There was very little to be happy about that day.

On my lunch break, when I was getting words in, I started to get doubts about the story I was working on. I had no reason to doubt the story, though. The narrative had been coming along nicely, but I got stuck in a section where I didn't know what would happen next.

My critical voice was yelling at me, and I started to second-guess the story. It was then that I realized that the only reason I was having a bad day was because of my mindset. My boss's email, while it put me in a bad mood, probably wouldn't have put me in a bad mood on any other day. There was just something about the universe that day that shifted my mindset in the wrong way. When I realized this, I immediately understood my mistakes.

First, I let my emotions cloud my judgment.

Second, my emotions dredged up my critical voice, which had free rein over my work until I realized what was happening.

Third, I went too far into the day without checking in with myself.

I can't honestly tell you that the rest of that day was great (it wasn't), but my writing was just fine. I pushed the negative thoughts aside, kept writing, and the next day, I discovered that what I wrote was good (at least in my opinion).

The most important thing you can do is divorce yourself from the idea that your critical voice knows what it's talking about. Often, it does not. When you listen to it, you will go astray.

I know, I know... That's easy to say but hard to do. But if you want to be prolific, you can't afford to get tangled up in your emotions and feelings of self-doubt. Self-doubt is one of the biggest challenges any writer faces, no matter how prolific they are. We all deal with it, but the most successful among us know how to recognize it and beat it away.

My strategies for conquering my critical voice are self-awareness, constant curiosity, and discipline. Whereas some writers would have been locked up in their emotions for days, weeks, or months, I snapped back in just a few hours. When I'm down, I don't stay down for long. That's the difference.

As I said, your emotions have far greater sway on your work than you realize. Therefore, you must learn to master your emotions. Do this and you will master yourself. Master yourself and you will become more prolific. Your writing will improve too.

Anyway, back to editing. All that stuff I just talked about?

That's a taste of what happens when you start your writing session with editing. You give your critical voice license to take control. Nothing good can ever come from that.

Don't misunderstand me. I'm not saying not to edit. I'm saying that you should focus on generating new words first, *especially* during your first writing session of the day. Write until you reach a natural stopping point, then decide if you want to pivot to editing. Or, save all your editing until your last writing session of the day. You'll have more words to show for it. You'll maintain a better mental state too.

Starting your writing sessions with *writing* is one of the healthiest things you can do.

The Dangers of Researching While Writing

(If you write historical fiction, just disregard this section. You're playing by a different set of rules and will have to do a lot more research than is suggested here.)

You should beware of research encroaching into your writing sessions.

Research is inevitable. There will always be times in your manuscript when you need to stop what you're doing and look something up. It's an occupational hazard.

Yes, I use the words "occupational hazard" deliberately. Sometimes, it can be easy to stop writing to research something, only to find yourself watching YouTube videos several hours later, with no words to show for your time.

Let's cover how you can avoid this problem.

There are two types of research: foundational research and just-in-time research.

Foundational research is research you must do before you start writing your story.

For example, if you want to write a book set in New York City, but you've never been to New York City, you've got a lot of work to do. However, you don't need to know *everything* about New York City to start writing your book. You only need to know the information leading up to the first chapter. That is, if you're a pantser. (Outliners do need to know more about the story, but it's still less than you think.)

Once you've started writing your novel, then you transition to just-in-time research. Just-in-time research is research that you need at the moment.

Say your character is going to a diner. You need to know what the diner looks like, so you do a web search for diners and try to find one in the style that you see in your mind's eye. Then, once you find that perfect match, you start writing again.

That's how just-in-time research works. You research things only when you need them.

Here's what most people do:

- They spend days, months, or years researching every little thing about a subject.
- They keep notebooks full of details, which takes an inordinate amount of time to prepare.
- When they're done with the novel, they will have used very little of what they researched.

Some writers argue that even if they don't use all their research, it helps them "learn" about the character, world, or story. I argue that "learning" doesn't mean anything if it doesn't lead to new words.

It's far better to segment your research into foundational research and just-in-time research.

Limit your foundational research to everything you need to know to write the first chapter. Also limit the amount of *time* you spend doing foundational research, and avoid the urge to procrastinate. Set a date when you will start your book, and start it on that date. Then, make just-in-time research your default research method.

When you practice just-in-time research, *everything* you research ends up in the book. It's more efficient.

Just as I recommended that you don't start your writing session with editing, you should also avoid starting writing sessions with research. Otherwise, you'll have procrastination working against you because there will always be something shiny to research. If you start writing early in the morning or late at night, you will also have tiredness and fatigue working against you.

When you're researching, there will always be another link that will take you to another page that will take you to another video that will take you to another book…and so on.

Therefore, do not start your writing sessions with research, especially your first session of the day. During your first session, doing just-in-time research is okay as long as you are disciplined about getting back to the page. Set a timer for five minutes, do your research, and return to your manuscript when the timer is up. If you can't find the answer to the issue you're solving in five minutes, I recommend writing down items that need to be researched and saving them for your *last* writing session of the day.

Don't write sloppy—write the best scene that you can and fill in anything you don't know with your imagination. Highlight those sections, research them, and correct them at the end of the day. Note that I said *at the end of the day*. Don't wait to research items or you'll forget about them.

But really, just do your just-in-time research and get back to the page. It makes your life easier in the end.

Fighting Procrastination

Let's say you follow my advice and start your writing sessions with fresh new words. The urge to procrastinate will strike. It always does, even for prolific writers.

Here's how it usually happens. You're writing a chapter in your book that you are unsure about, not passionate about, or you're not enjoying. (Remember what I said about the critical voice.) As you progress, the words get harder to write. Subconsciously, you check out. The next thing you know, you're surfing the internet and have nothing to show for your session.

It happens to all of us.

Here are some tips to beat procrastination:

1. If you aren't feeling the current scene you're writing, write through it quickly. Not sloppily, but quickly. Later, you'll probably find that there was nothing wrong with the scene at all.
2. The longer you take to write a scene, the longer it takes you to get to the next scene.
3. Find ways to keep yourself motivated. Think about the chapters that come next. If you're goal motivated, like me, you will find a way to get there.

4. One word at a time is the only way to get through some chapters. When in doubt, write the next word, even if you don't know what it will be. Follow your fingers.
5. Technology won't save you. The sad reality is that if you can't focus, technology isn't going to help you. You must develop mental discipline. To develop that discipline, you must know your goals and align your activities with them so that reaching your goals each day is a foregone conclusion.

Here's another truth: sometimes, procrastination can be your friend.

I've put off writing chapters for a few hours, only to come across an inspiration that ended up in my next writing session. That's okay too, as long as you don't make excuses. Whenever I decide to walk away from a chapter, it's only for a few hours, never more. I always strive to hit my quota for that day (and I usually do), and I don't linger for long in any area of my books. I keep things moving forward. You should too.

Common Procrastination Points

The urge to procrastinate is common in every novel, but there are certain danger points where it happens more often:

- starting the book
- the one-third mark, and
- the two-thirds mark

For some, starting a book is daunting. No one likes to stare at a blinking cursor. If you need help, visualize the first scene in the story and why the hero is there, and then start writing.

That's not always easy, but it is a surefire way to get the novel started.

The one-third mark is the most dangerous part of any book. It occurs around the 25 to 33 percent mark, and it's the point when many writers abandon their work. This is because most writers start their books in a blaze of glory. The writing is fun, they love the story and the characters, and everything is going well. I call this the "honeymoon phase."

Once the honeymoon phase is over, fear sets in. The writer begins to doubt their work and the story's viability.

I have a theory about the one-third mark. This is the area where many elements converge. The hero has usually passed the point of no return and met the other supporting characters and villains. Plot lines tend to merge around this point, and the writer has to figure out how to orchestrate everything. To use an analogy, the writer has set the table, but now they have to start serving the meal.

To use another analogy, the one-third mark is a literary traffic jam.

Have you ever been stuck in a traffic jam that existed for no reason? You inch along bumper-to-bumper for several miles only to find that the traffic jam clears. There was no accident, stalled car, or construction—just an out-of-the-blue traffic jam because too many cars were on the road. The one-third mark of your novel is like that.

The two-thirds mark of the novel is like the one-third mark, but it's the preparation for the end. This problem spot usually occurs around the 65 to 75 percent mark. The problem with the one-third mark is orchestrating all the novel's elements, but the problem with the two-thirds mark is wrapping them up.

With the two-thirds mark, you'll fight boredom and fatigue. You may already know what's going to happen, and your creative voice wants to race off to the land of the next story, resulting in boredom. Or, you may be exhausted from getting this far and want the damn book to be done already.

The best way to tackle the two-thirds mark is—wait for it—keep writing. One word, one sentence, one chapter at a time. Keep your head down and do the work. Eventually, you'll look up and you'll be done.

Here's another tip about the one-third and two-thirds marks: these "trouble spots" don't last long—a few thousand words at best. If you power through those words, the trouble will clear and you'll usually look back and wonder why you were feeling uncertain in the first place.

Finding the Picture of Good

What does a good day look like for you?

The only way to be prolific is to write new words every day, but that's not the only thing you have to do in your writing business.

You've also got to market, hire cover designers and editors, format your books, keep track of your expenses and income for tax purposes, answer emails, and myriad other things. All of these tasks compete with your writing, and if you don't do them, you won't have a writing career.

This is another drag on your productivity that you must be aware of and plan for. You can't make money if you don't run your writing business properly!

Early in my career, I fell into the trap of prioritizing words over all else. This meant that if I had only one hour per day to move my writing business forward, I chose to write words. That was a great choice because I have a big portfolio to show for it, but it came at a cost: I did very little marketing early in my career.

Perhaps if I had marketed more, I would have made more money. I chose to advance my craft and solve the productivity problem first. My hunch was that the money would come later. I was right, but I did pay a price.

You'll have to figure out how to constantly balance writing new words with all the other responsibilities of being a writer in today's age. It's not easy, but it can be done. You can be successful in achieving your word counts as well as in marketing and business, even if you aren't a full-time writer. The secret is to determine "the picture of good" for every day.

To determine your picture of good, ask yourself: do you want to prioritize words, or do you want a more balanced approach, juggling writing, marketing, and business?

I like to think about this as a "you pick two" puzzle. In the business world, it's a mantra that a customer must choose between three elements: speed, quality, and price. They can only pick two.

You can get a high-quality product quickly, but it will cost you. You can get a high-quality cheap product, but it's going to take a while.

You get the picture.

In your career as a writer, you can pick two skills to master, but you will always be lacking in the third:

- You can choose to be a fast writer and be good at business, but that will come at the expense of marketing.
- You can be a fast writer and a good marketer, but it will come at the expense of the business.
- You can be a savvy marketer and good at business, but it will come at the expense of your writing.

Is this true for everyone? No, but it's a good rule of thumb, and you can usually see it at work with any writer you look at.

You're reading this book, so you've chosen writing as one of your strengths. What is your other strength?

Once you've chosen your focus areas, you can design your day appropriately.

Let's say you want to focus on writing and business. You'll need to accomplish new words each day, as well as at least one business item. That might be staying up to date on your taxes, finding new tax deductions, or anything else related to running a savvy publishing business.

Let's say that you want to focus on writing and marketing. You should accomplish new words each day, as well as progress in your marketing.

You'll need to find ways to work in the remaining area as time allows. You can't *not* ever do anything in this area, but it will be less of a priority because your time is limited. As you become more successful, you'll find more time to incorporate more tasks into your daily writing activities.

I have chosen writing and business as my main focus areas. I market when I can. It's worked out pretty well for me so far in my career, but it does mean that I sometimes leave money on the table. I've learned to be okay with that.

New Words, New Words, New Words

I've repeated myself enough by now, but I'll say it a final time: begin your writing sessions with new words!

There's a time and a place for editing, research, and even procrastination, honestly. But the best thing you can do is keep putting words on the page.

Here's my only word of caution: you also want to balance your writing and editing. Don't write so many words that you can't edit them fast enough. That will slow you down as well.

Ideally, you'll want to find balance. Figure out how long it takes you to write and edit 1,000 words.

Let's say that it takes you 30 minutes to write 1,000 words. Super.

It takes you 30 minutes to edit those words. Great.

If you have a two-hour writing session, spend 30 minutes writing, 30 minutes editing, then 30 minutes writing, and 30 minutes editing. When done right, you'll finish your session "neat," which means that you don't have any editing left to do. This means you can start the next day fresh, with new words. It doesn't always work out this way practically, but as long as you don't leave too many words left to edit the next day, you're doing it correctly. However, your goal should be to end every day clean when you can.

Plus, ending the day fresh is an amazing feeling, especially when you hit your goal for the day!

R.A.M.P.ing Up Your Career

Next, I recommend developing a productivity acronym that you can remember that spells out what you should be doing every day.

My acronym is R.A.M.P. It stands for reading, data analysis, marketing, and production. This is my personal acronym. It doesn't have to be yours, especially if you are really pressed for time. You may want something shorter. I share mine to help you think about your day.

R is for reading. To keep my creative well full, I need to keep reading. Reading ensures a steady stream of ideas into my mind, and it keeps me exposed to new things. It's much easier to stay inspired. **Therefore, a good day for me is any day where I have read (or listened to) at least one chapter of a book.**

A is for analysis of data. Data is important to me as a writer because it is how I uncover opportunities. I prioritize using data whenever possible to make decisions about my writing.

Examples of using data to uncover opportunities include:

- reviewing my daily word counts and using data to improve them
- reviewing how many edits I received from my editor and determining how to decrease my edits over time
- reviewing sales data to look for trends
- reviewing industry data to determine trends in my genre or things to watch out for

And that's just scratching the surface. When you look for data, it reveals itself to you in interesting ways. I spend a great deal of time in Microsoft Excel and digging through data sets. That makes me unique among writers, but serves my overall strategy to be a technology and data-driven writer.

A good day for me is any day where I glean insight from data about how to improve my writing business in some way.

M is for marketing. I can't grow my writing business if I don't market regularly. As I said before, I spent a great deal of time early in my career *not* marketing. I am making up for it now by incorporating it into my daily workflow. **A good day for me is any day where I've done at least one marketing task, however small.**

Examples of marketing tasks include:

- ordering or designing a book cover, or moving a current book cover order forward by providing feedback to a designer
- setting up new Amazon, BookBub, or Facebook ads
- booking advertising promos
- building my email list
- adjusting the prices of my books
- collaborating with another author
- giving a podcast interview
- performing a speaking engagement

And more. Marketing is a universe of activities, and you can always do something to move your marketing forward. Little activities add up in a big way over a year.

P is for the production of words. In other words, my daily word count. How much did I write? Did I hit my quota? This is the most important letter and where I spend the majority of my time each day, but it's the last letter in the acronym because I want to make sure I don't lose sight of the other elements.

Writing will always demand the most of your time. It is the biggest attention hog in your day, or at least it should be. However, I build a more balanced writing career by focusing on other daily activities.

You should strive for balance too. If not, here's what will happen:

- You will write so fast that your fingers almost fall off.
- You will fall behind in every other area of your writing business (like emails, taxes, or marketing).
- You will stop writing to catch up in those other areas.
- Your productivity will suffer.

It's far better to make a little progress in the areas that matter at the expense of a slight reduction in your word count. Trust me.

A good day for me is any day where I manage to hit my writing quota.

Do everything you can to stay balanced. It will make you a more productive writer, even if you have to slow down just a little bit. This life is a marathon, not a sprint. When you sprint, you have to cool down afterward. The cooling down is what hurts your productivity.

. . .

The Realities of R.A.M.P.

I wish I could tell you that I adhere to R.A.M.P. every day. I do not. But most days, I accomplish at least two of the letters.

Developing a productivity acronym is aspirational. It gives you something to shoot for. I don't beat myself up if I don't achieve it. I just try again the next day. Most days, I am successful, though.

If something doesn't fall neatly within R.A.M.P., it's not a priority for me.

Maybe your acronym is only two letters. Whatever works best for you. But give yourself a "picture of good" to strive for every day. Verbalize it. Write it down. When you do, you'll find that you magically achieve it.

Outlining Secrets

I'm back to grind my ax into a fine nub on outlining.

Ah, outlining. Many authors do it. I argue that it makes you a less efficient writer.

There are two types of writers: plotters and pantsers. Plotters need to outline before writing their story. Pantsers jump into the story and feel their way through it.

I am firmly in the pantsing camp. I love it so much that I wrote a book called *The Pocket Guide to Pantsing: How to Write a Novel Without an Outline (with Confidence)*. It is a comprehensive guide to this writing method. I share that so you know where my sympathies lie, but I also have advice for plotters.

I outlined my first ten novels. I also published a video on YouTube called "How to Outline a Novel in 10 Ways" that is, to this day, one of the most popular videos on my channel with over 100,000 views, even though I don't outline anymore. I've used most of the major methods, and I understand outlining well.

Here's the thing about outlining: it *is* inefficient. Let's put aside whether outlining is helpful for you or not, just for a little while. I'm only talking about the process.

Here's how outlining usually works:

- You write your outline.
- You start writing your book.
- At some point, you deviate from your outline, rendering the outline less effective, especially if you don't update it.
- At some point, the outline doesn't help you because it's not granular enough or you get into a situation you didn't plan for; therefore, you deviate again.
- When you're done writing the novel, it will differ substantially from what you outlined.

Some people stick to their outlines without straying from them, but I would bet that most people do not. If you have to deviate from your outline, that is the definition of inefficiency.

Think about it. You spent all this time thinking about what was going to happen in your story, and then you didn't follow the plan. Somewhere along the way, something went wrong.

Now, let's bring helpfulness back into the conversation—I recognize that some people find outlines helpful in getting started with the story. I won't deny that, but if anything I wrote previously resonates with you, you can't deny that outlining creates hindrances in your process.

As partial as I am to pantsing, no writing method is perfect or *completely* inefficient:

•Outlining's biggest problem is that you may not actually use most of your outline.

•Pantsing's biggest problem is that you may venture into rabbit holes.

But let me explain why I still prefer pantsing.

When you write without an outline, you simply start writing. You sit down at the writing desk and type the story. You don't know what will happen, so you make it up as you go and adjust any plot holes that come up *as they come up*. Yes, you will venture down rabbit holes, but I find that it doesn't happen that often. When it does, I just delete the unneeded words, back up, and start where things went off the rails. At most, this is usually a few hundred words for me. Occasionally it will creep over the thousand-word mark. If I write 3,000 words per hour and I throw away 1,000 words, that represents 20 minutes wasted. If I outlined a novel correctly, it would have probably taken me longer than 20 minutes to outline those words. But that's just me.

Why the Term "Writing Without an Outline" is Actually a Misnomer

It's not technically true that pantsers don't outline. At least, not if they do it correctly. If you follow my methods in *The Pocket Guide to Pantsing* or Dean Wesley Smith's book *Writing into the Dark*, then you *outline as you go*.

An outline that you create as you go is called a reverse outline. In a reverse outline, you write down what happens in the story as it happens. I keep a Microsoft Excel spreadsheet that I update every time I finish a chapter that contains the chapter number, the point of view character, a summary of what happens, and the characters present. Any time I need to remember what happened in the story, I refer to the outline. Because it is a spreadsheet, I can filter it.

A reverse outline is more efficient because *everything in the outline is everything in the story*. It is always 100 percent up to date. As I said, if you have questions about what you wrote previously while you're writing the novel, you can refer to the outline. You can refer to the outline if you have questions about what happened in the novel several years later. Therefore, the outline becomes a useful historical document for you. This is immensely helpful if you write a series, leave it for a few years, and come back to it.

This is not necessarily true if you outline before you start writing. I imagine that most people who outline before writing never go back and update their outlines. Therefore, any inconsistencies between the outline and the text represent a waste of time. This is not the case with reverse outlining, and a major reason why pantsing can help you become a more efficient writer.

If I've persuaded you, awesome. It was part of my evil plan to create more pantsers in the world...

But okay, I'm done bashing outlining. You may have read everything in this chapter and still said to yourself, "That's great, but I am not going to become a pantser."

No problem. Let's talk about how to make your outlining more efficient too.

Tips for Outliners

I want you to think about the last book you outlined. Do this exercise:

- Get your outline.
- Get the finished version of your book.
- Compare the outline to the finished version of your book and note the differences.
- Count how many chapters had differences, and estimate what percentage of the original outline was accurate.
- Ask yourself how you could do better next time.

Let's say that you deviated from the outline in 50 percent of your chapters. Why did you deviate? What did you change? Is there anything you can learn from this? Perhaps you weren't thorough enough in describing the setting. Or, you decided to go a different direction but forgot to update the other areas of your outline. Do the work and get the data.

This will be painful, but I promise it will make you more efficient. When you understand why your outline failed, you can use that knowledge to make your next outline more accurate. If you deviated from the outline in 50 percent of your chapters and you decrease the deviations with your next novel to 25 percent, that's a major win.

Next, most importantly, update your outline any time you deviate from it. Doing this will take time, but you'll thank me later.

If you're an outliner, my message is to commit to finding ways to spend less time outlining and creating higher-quality outlines. If you dare, eschew outlining altogether. It will make you a faster and more efficient writer.

If you still have questions about this, I recommend checking out my book *The Pocket Guide to Pantsing*. It will hold your hand and get you comfortable with pantsing.

Editing Secrets

I discussed writing sloppy in the first *Be a Writing Machine* and why it is a bad idea. I want to explore this further.

How much time do you spend editing? This is another thing you should track. Painful, I know, but this will be an illuminating exercise.

Many writers I know spend a decent amount of time drafting their work, but then spend multiple times more editing the work. We've talked before about the relationship between writing and editing—editing is a drag on your time.

Therefore, find ways to make your editing more efficient. How many drafts do you do before you mark the book as complete? Let's say that you do ten drafts. Do you really need all those drafts, or could you do it in eight drafts next time?

Once you accomplish eight drafts, can you cut that down to five?

I am a one-draft writer, but that's a misnomer. Because I loop through my novels, I technically am writing them in multiple drafts, but I'm doing it as I go as opposed to the writer who writes multiple drafts one after the other. I don't do any rewriting—just subtle revising here and there.

(Rewriting is another topic altogether. It kills your productivity…Very inefficient.)

Remember the law of diminishing returns. After a certain point, your draft isn't going to get better. It might get worse. This is another area where self-doubt will creep into your life. You should examine why if you take many drafts to finish your novel.

I used to be a five-draft writer. Once I discovered how much time I was wasting, I became a three-draft writer. Now I'm a one-draft writer. You can do it too, and you can do it without skimping on your quality. Don't let naysayers talk you out of it. **One-draft writing simply means that you slow down and focus on getting the story right the first time.**

Note that I said slow down… Haven't I been saying throughout this book that you should *increase* your word count? I know it sounds like an oxymoron, but by slowing down and focusing on getting the story right the first time, you will save hours upon hours of editing. Any speed you sacrifice is made up for by the shortened length of time it will take you to write the book. Funny how that works.

Many of the classic pulp writers were one-draft writers. If they did it with *typewriters and white-out*, we can do it with our word processors, no problem.

Beware the Myths Around "Hacks"

Myths abound about fast writing. Writers who write fast are frequently called "hacks." I find the term incredibly insulting.

First, let's set aside people who write really fast and publish books full of typos and errors. I never advocate for that. If you read the rest of my books for writers, I make this very clear and I frequently recommend editing tips for writers. We can both agree that you shouldn't publish work that is unedited or sloppily put together.

The trouble is with authors who are fast and *good*.

There's a stigma in our society that authors who don't take an ungodly amount of time to produce their books are hacks. That's bullshit. These myths are usually perpetuated by academics, snobs who think that commercial fiction is for the masses, and by authors who get indoctrinated by such lies.

I've never much cared about what some academic in a high tower thinks about my work. They're never going to read it anyway. I've also never cared about garnering praise from someone who holds a romanticized view of how writing *should* be, and who has probably never written a novel themselves.

Instead, I focus on reality and pay attention to what the best practitioners in the craft are doing. Those practitioners happen to be the writers that snobs call "hacks." You know, the mega bestsellers who have sold millions of books. Those hacks.

You need a reality check if you think someone like James Patterson is a hack. Any author who is selling that many books is someone to study because they're doing almost everything right.

To name a few things:

- He's prolific.
- He writes books (solo and with others) rain or shine.
- He's an excellent writer.
- He creates amazing characters and plots.
- He's fast and good, whether you like his work or not.

Millions of readers aren't wrong. To call James Patterson (or any mega bestseller) a hack is incredibly insulting to those readers who like him. Like him or hate him, you can't deny that he's got world-class talent, and he's one of the best writers in the world. The same goes for other big-name authors.

The moment you understand this, then you will see writing differently. You'll stop romanticizing the way things *should be* and you'll see them for how they are. And when you see things for how they are, you can start replicating the masters.

Only the masters matter. No one else.

If someone thinks I'm a hack or a terrible person because of how I work, I don't care. In the meantime, while they're complaining about me, I'll be selling books, building a community of readers who love my work, and reaping the benefits. People who hold such negative views of other people usually view themselves in the same way. Their words and actions are merely projections. Such negative energy only hurts them in the end.

But, I can hear the critics now..."But, Michael, you're not James Patterson. What if your books are no good? What if they don't sell?"

I don't place my self-worth on success. Doing the work for me is enough. So, while critics use sales and perceived quality as a metric to bash fast writers, I choose not to play that game. I just let the critics sit in a dark room and shout to the few people who want to listen to them.

If I finish a book, I put it out into the world and see what happens. Sometimes, my books fail. But every book teaches me something that I can use for the next one.

Plus, the beauty of books is that anything can happen. You might publish a book that goes nowhere today, but the landscape in your genre could change in a few years and the book could find new life.

Here's another secret about being a fast writer...if you write a bad book, no one will ever know because they won't buy it...

Here's another secret: if you write a book quickly (and well), and no one buys it or it doesn't meet your sales expectations, you're only out the time you spent on it. If you write a book in a month, you're out a month. Now, keep in mind that you should be thinking long-term. Let's say that your writing career spans 50 years. One month represents 0.0017 percent of your career. Not that big of a deal when you think about it that way.

But let's say you take two years to write a book and it still flops. That book represents 4 percent of your career. And hell, if you're taking two years to write books, you might only write 25 books in your lifetime…if you write that many. So the math gets worse, actually.

We should also explore the other side of this argument. If you write a book quickly (and well) and readers love it, that's amazing! You just hit the jackpot. The truth is, if you follow the techniques in this book and commit to becoming a better, faster, and more efficient writer, you will increase your odds. Even if lightning never strikes (which it never does for most of us), you'll still fail your way to success.

Creativity breeds creativity. The more you write, the better you get. As long as you keep at it and keep improving, it's impossible not to write a book that readers will love. The only variable is how long it will take you. We all have different paths.

Again, I'm not saying that you should write sloppy, publish unedited work, or be a terrible writer. **You must strive to be among the very best. By doing so, you'll find that readers are quite forgiving as long as you're doing your damndest to entertain them.**

Therefore, you should separate yourself from romanticized views of the writing lifestyle. Your writing life is what you make it. You *cannot* care about what other people think about your writing process. You shouldn't care about what other people think about your writing either.

Write fast, write well, and be prolific. And remember that editing, while essential for any manuscript, isn't the place where you should sink all your time.

A Revised Opinion on Beta Readers

In the first *Be a Writing Machine*, I wrote this about beta readers: "Beta readers: bless their hearts, but you don't need them."

I explained that beta reading creates a bottleneck in your writing process. You must be extremely organized and good at making sure that they hit your deadlines. They pose an efficiency risk in that you may find yourself waiting around for feedback for a long time.

There are ways around this (and I have covered the best way to engage beta readers and keep them motivated in my book *The Self-Publishing Advice Compendium*), but I argued that most people don't really need them. I still believe that's true, but I've revised my opinion to add some nuance. I've been using beta readers, but in a very specific way that is a little counterintuitive.

Here's the problem with betas: they are another way that writers soothe their self-doubt. Writers think their story is not good enough, so they outsource their doubt to someone who will save the day. I still think that's a terrible idea. You must learn to develop a backbone and stand by your story.

If you work with a beta reader, you do so to strengthen the story. Not because you don't think it's good enough. But there is a difference between "I'm recruiting beta readers to help me fix the story" and "I'm recruiting beta readers to help me strengthen what I have." A world of difference. With the former, you're going to ask beta readers to look for everything wrong, which they will almost certainly find (and you will be all too happy to agree with them); with the latter, you ask for their advice but you have the courage to discard anything that doesn't suit your story. With the latter, you remain in control, and that's critical. But that requires an iron will.

Instead, I suggest you avoid both of those polarities and think about beta readers differently. I view beta readers as people who can help me validate my research. I call them "fact-checkers" instead. Rather than viewing beta readers as a function of *editing*, you'll get much better results and be far more efficient with them if you view them as a function of *research*.

Let me explain.

Improving Your Research with Fact-Checkers

I have been experimenting with fact-checking my research in recent novels. It's one thing to research subject matter in your book, but another thing entirely to verify that your research is accurate.

Every novel I write has about two or three subject matter areas that I need help with. One novel in particular (*Dead Rat Walking*, The Chicago Rat Shifter Book 1) took place in a city that I don't live in, featured an animal that I was not familiar with, and featured a sibling relationship, which was new territory for me. I did as much research as I could, but I had this nagging feeling that I needed to have someone look at the novel to verify if what I wrote made sense.

This is where the concept of fact-checking comes in. You

recruit several people to evaluate what you have written to verify if you executed properly on your research. Nothing more, nothing less.

You can research a topic until you know it inside out, but there's a difference between knowing something well and writing it accurately. Fact-checkers test your skill as a writer.

With this novel, I recruited three different groups of fact-checkers: one group who live or had lived in the city of Chicago for a very long time and were familiar with it; another group who were familiar with rodent biology, and who had degrees in biology or bioengineering; and a final group who were female fantasy readers who had younger brothers and who had given them relationship advice (something that happens in the novel with my main character and his sister).

I explained to the fact-checkers what I was looking for, and I gave them basic instructions. Then I sent them excerpts from the novel that contained only the items that needed to be fact-checked. For example, I sent my Chicago fact-checkers only the sections about Chicago, my biology fact-checkers only the sections about rats, and my female readers only the chapters from the point of view of the hero's sister (who features prominently in the story). It was a little awkward sending them only parts of the novel, but I believe this was more respectful of their time. It also allowed them to get through comments much faster. Most of the fact-checkers took less than a week to provide their feedback.

I believe that, ultimately, readers decide the merits of the story, but I want to do all I can to make sure that they have an enjoyable reading experience and that little technical details don't pull them out of the story. In fact, if I can get these technical details right, it will enhance readers' enjoyment of the story. It will strengthen what I have already written.

This technique was inspired by mega bestseller Arthur Hailey, who was a household name in the 1960s and 1970s. Many of his novels topped *the New York Times* bestseller list.

I am a big fan of Arthur Hailey and consider him to be one of my all-time favorites. I was pleasantly surprised when I discovered that his wife, Sheila, wrote a biography of how she met him and their marriage. The biography talked about Arthur's writing process and how he researched his novels. His novels take place in a single setting such as an airport, hotel, bank, or auto factory, and it features thriller plots from the perspective of the employees who work there. When you read his novels, you get the sense that he has meticulously researched every element. Fortunately, Sheila talked about his process in the book. She mentioned how he took copious notes, read as many books as he could about the topics he needed to research, and even conducted field interviews with industry experts (I imagine that being a *New York Times* bestseller will open a lot of doors with industry executives). For his book *Wheels*, he worked on an assembly line for a few hours to understand line workers. He would take pages and pages of notes, organize them using a notecard system, and then incorporate his research into his novels as he wrote.

Reading about his thought process got me thinking about my research process. I write science fiction and fantasy, so the level of research I need to do is not as substantial as Arthur Hailey's, but good research is a bedrock of good fiction.

The feedback my fact-checkers gave me was amazing. Not only did they answer the questions that I posed to them in good detail, but they also described how they think about certain issues, which was more helpful than the actual feedback they provided. I found that learning how someone thinks about something and why they think the way they do is an underrated window into writing more engaging characters. For example, my Chicago fact-checkers had very strong opinions about certain things in the city, such as gentrification.

When you can get inside people's heads, you can exercise mind control on the page because you can go deeper into an issue or explore different perspectives of an issue that readers haven't considered, lending more authenticity to the novel. That's gold for a fiction writer. It also shows the reader you did your homework.

To find my fact-checkers, I used my network and asked for help on my podcasts and daily blog. Several of my readers reached out offering help, which was humbling. I also found fact-checkers on Upwork.com. I posted a job with a description of what I needed with a small budget and a one-week turn-around, and I screened applicants based on their experience and responses to interview questions in the job description. My Chicago fact-checking job attracted almost 70 people who lived in the city or were very familiar with it.

In short, it's not hard to find people who have the experience you need. You just need to ask for it.

If you still want to recruit a beta reader to read your whole novel, weave fact-checking into their responsibilities and make that their key focus. I believe the beta readers' life experience is an underrated resource that writers don't tap into.

Beta readers are not just readers; they are parents, professionals in an industry, members of their community, and so on. They have hobbies other than reading and unique perspectives on life that they are willing to share if you ask them. When you lead by asking for these types of experiences, you can attract higher-quality people to help you with your story. Let's say you have a fantasy novel with religious overtones based on Judaism. Why not look for a fantasy reader who is a devout follower of the Jewish religion and deeply involved in their synagogue and the Jewish community as one of your *beta readers*? Most people don't think about that; they just want to find anyone and everyone willing to beta read for them, missing out on their life experiences.

I think it is better to have beta readers with the experience you're looking for than generic beta readers who will read anything. For example, I no longer recruit beta readers who don't exclusively read in the genre I write in. A reader who is well-versed in the genre always gives better feedback than someone who "just likes to read everything." To take this further, someone who reads in your genre and has experience in the areas you write about will always be better. More importantly, they will be more engaged and give you better feedback. They'll also meet your deadlines...improving your efficiency.

And if you pay your beta readers, you'll attract the best quality people who will deliver feedback on time and with passion.

I enjoyed the fact-checking process so much that I have decided to make it a part of all of my novels moving forward. It has made a measurable difference in the quality of my writing.

So to revise my statements on this...Beta readers: God bless them, but you don't need them. If you use them, treat them as fact-checkers instead, send them excerpts of the novel, and tap into their life experience to get better feedback, motivate them, and keep your project on schedule.

Advanced Strategies to Beat
Writer's Block

How good are you at generating ideas? When it's time to write a new book, do you struggle to figure out what to write next? Or, do you have so many ideas that you will never get to them all?

I know writers in both camps. If you want to be prolific, you want to put yourself in the second camp. Your goal should be to have so many ideas that you will die before you write them all. To do that, you must keep your creative well deep and full.

If you've never thought about how you generate ideas, I encourage you to do so.

Do you keep all those new ideas in your head, or do you write them down? If you keep them in your head, you're more likely to forget them.

You should write your ideas down. How you record your ideas is up to you, but I'll give you a few ideas.

Capture Ideas with a Note-Taking App

. . .

There are dozens of note-taking apps on the market. Examples include Evernote, Microsoft OneNote, and Bear. With so many choices, you're guaranteed to find one that will meet your needs. These apps have web clipper browser extensions that let you save content from the internet into a digital notebook.

Let's say you come across an article with a picture of a castle that inspires you. Click the web clipper, save it to your notebook, and it will be there the next time you need inspiration.

Over the years, I have built dozens of notebooks and thousands of pages of notes containing random things that moved me. I frequently save things for a later day. In fact, I save things and immediately forget about them, only to discover them years later when I'm digging through my notebooks.

I don't organize my notebooks; I leave them messy on purpose. I do this because of the concept of "idea sex." In her book *Become an Idea Machine: Because Ideas Are the Currency of the 21st Century*, Claudia Azula Altucher explains that when you capture ideas, they tend to merge together into new ones. She calls this process "idea sex."

I like to think that my ideas are having sex all the time. For example, let's say that I save a picture of a cyberpunk version of Super Mario inspired by the 1993 film. I see that image next to an article about African mythology. What if I wrote a book about a hero living in a cyberpunk world who gets transported to a mythological world? That would be interesting.

An alternative to this process is simply carrying around a physical notebook with you to capture your ideas. Any time you come up with an idea, write it down. The only downside to a physical notebook is that you can lose it or it can be destroyed in a fire or natural disaster. But do whatever suits you.

Develop a Process for Capturing Ideas Quickly

. . .

When you come up with an idea, you must capture it as soon as possible. This is critical.

Write it down, record a voice memo, take a picture, draw a crude illustration—it doesn't matter. Capture it!

The sooner you capture ideas in their rawest form, the more useful they will be for you when you need them.

Also, consider taking this advanced tip: prepare the ideas for easy merging into a novel. Let's say that you walk into a bar that inspires you. Maybe the decor is unique, or the patrons at the bar are fodder for a novel.

We all know the common advice for writers: write in the five senses. After all, if you use the five senses, then that will make your work more vivid. When you capture your idea, if possible, capture it in the five senses. This will make it much easier for you to "import" the idea into your work in all five dimensions.

Man, when I started doing this, it took my ideas to the next level. It's amazing how much you forget about a place even a few hours after you leave. You tend to remember what you *see*. Smell, hear, touch, and taste? Not so much.

By doing this, you will train your writer's eye to think in terms of the five senses, which will make your writing more vivid. It will also make you more observant.

Keep capturing ideas well; over time, you will develop robust notebooks that will be there for you if you can't decide what to write next. Fortunately, I rarely need my notebooks, but they're a good insurance policy for me.

Be a Student of People

When new writers ask me what they can do to improve their craft, I always tell them to be a student of people. It's fundamental to fiction writing.

Being a student of people means putting yourself in places where you can watch them. Coffee shops, grocery stores, gas stations, airports—wherever people are, you can watch them.

The next time you're in public, pick one random person and watch them. Don't be a stalker, please, and don't be creepy...

But let's say you're at the grocery store and there's a man in front of you in the checkout line. Maybe he's in dusty construction clothes. What's his story? More importantly, how might you write him into one of your books? If it were me, I'd first try to get a sense of the person's energy. Is he calm? Frantic to get through checkout? Constantly on his phone and distracted?

Next, I'd pay attention to his clothes and appearance—the dust on the man's shirt or the mole under his left eye, for example.

Last, I'd pay attention to the words he uses when he speaks, and how. Sometimes, I might even write down what he says, like if he has a unique accent and says something unusual.

When you're observing people, ask yourself how you would write this person into your story. That simple question is the gateway to writing better fiction and nonfiction because it trains your brain to translate people onto the page. The best part about this exercise is that there are no wrong answers. You don't have to be right—you're just practicing and stretching your mind.

Collect Words Like Pokémon

Collect interesting words. This will help you expand your vocabulary so you can write more compelling imagery, which will help you when you capture ideas.

Use pen and paper or a note-taking app like Evernote to write down unique words whenever you encounter them.

Now, you can go overboard here. Don't go off collecting rare words that no one will ever know, the Latin names of flowers, or things like that. The point is not to make the reader reach for a dictionary. They don't like that. (If you write literary fiction, that's a different story.)

The key is to expand the vocabulary that your readers will understand. Chances are, there are simple words that you don't immediately think of, but that can expand your vocabulary and make a big impact on your writing.

I read a poem once where the poet used the phrase "police cars cockroaching through tunnels." The imagery was completely unexpected, but it always stuck with me because it was so vivid.

That's why reading good books is so important—bestsellers often use arresting and unexpected word choices. Poetry is also another great source of fun and interesting words.

Create a repository of words in one long document and review it every once in a while. I think you'll find fun and unique opportunities to use perfect words that your readers won't expect, but will find delight in.

Mix Ideas Around and Review Them Regularly

Mix your ideas around. If you've followed the previous few tips, you'll collect many ideas very quickly.

What do you do with them?

Every once in a while, I like to go into my idea book and review all the ideas I have. I scroll through them randomly with no real agenda. What I find is that things start jumping out at me. An idea I captured yesterday might merge with an idea I captured three years ago and create a unique synthesis.

For example, back in 2011, I reread *Treasure Island* by Robert Louis Stevenson, one of my favorite books. I absolutely love Long John Silver. I always thought it would be interesting to write a Long John-inspired character myself someday.

In 2015, I happened upon some amazing dragon images on Pinterest, one in particular of an enormous black dragon. I also read Shakespeare's *Richard III* that year. Somehow, I got the idea to write a story with an evil dragon antihero whose personality was one part Long John Silver and one part Richard III. That character became the hero in my *Last Dragon Lord* series, which is one of my most popular fantasy series with readers—available in e-book, paperback, and audio.

Mix your ideas around and you'll be surprised at what might happen.

Treat the Authors of the Books You Read Like Mentors

One of my favorite TED Talks is from an entrepreneur named Tai Lopez. Lopez went from poor to rich, and he credits reading as one of the reasons. He imagined the books he read as mentors. Every book was an opportunity to learn a life lesson.

Lopez is a controversial figure. He loves women, fast cars, and money, and his personality is not for everyone. But I like the advice.

If you treated every book you read like a mentor, what could you learn? How might you level up your craft?

Commit to Reading Outside Your Comfort Zone

. . .

Expand your mind. If you normally read fantasy, consider reading horror. Read some popular nonfiction. You'll learn something.

I've always believed that reading makes writers more empathetic. Reading outside your comfort zone exposes you to authors and stories you have never seen or heard of. That is *always* a good thing.

Commit to Rereading Your Favorite Books on Occasion

My uncle's favorite book is *Great Expectations*. He rereads it every couple of years.

Why not reread some of your favorite books on occasion? What might you learn from a new reading that you didn't see the first time around from a craft perspective?

Creativity Breeds Creativity

Many people think that writing faster will force them to run out of ideas. They envisage a day when they simply have no more ideas. Maybe that's true for some, but writing faster has led to even more ideas for me. The faster I write, the more ideas I generate.

In other words, creativity breeds creativity. Don't be afraid of it. If you've been reading this book and wondering if the methods will lead you to the "empty" path one day, you're right to be concerned, but if you follow the tips in this chapter, it shouldn't happen.

As I said, I've been writing at least 10 books per year every year without fail, and I've yet to finish a book with no clue what to write next.

So much of creativity and keeping the well full involves faith and courage. You've got to have faith that your methods are contributing to the well. You've also got to have the courage to blaze into new stories with the trust that the next idea will always be there.

Next Steps

You made it (again)!

I hope the techniques in this book will help you, wherever you are in your writing journey, whatever your goals may be.

Even if the techniques in this book help you write just a few more words per day, I consider that a victory. If they explode your word count…well, that's a game changer!

I've learned so much since the first *Be a Writing Machine* that I couldn't wait to write this one. I view the writing journey as one that never truly ends. You always keep learning. I'm excited about where your journeys will take you and I hope this book plays a small part in helping you walk the path you want.

I covered a lot in this book and I have more books that dive into deeper detail:

1. *The Indie Author Bestiary I & II: An Epic Quest Against the Beasts of the Writing World* will help you beat self-doubt and all the other emotional blocks you face as a writer.
2. *The Writing App Handbook: How to Choose the Best App for Fiction and Nonfiction Writing* will help you find your perfect writing app match.

3. *How to Dictate a Book: The Author's Guide to Effortless Dictation* will teach you how to dictate like a pro and explode your word counts.
4. *The Pocket Guide to Pantsing: How to Write a Novel Without an Outline (with Confidence)* will teach you how to master pantsing once and for all.
5. *Advanced Author Editing: Creating Cleaner Manuscripts* is an advanced book that will help you get cleaner drafts the first time around.
6. *Indie Author Confidential* is a quarterly series where I document my journey as a writer. It's a behind-the-scenes look at my life as a working writer.

I hope these books will help you write smarter and faster, beat writer's block, and be prolific!

I also have a YouTube channel called Author Level Up. I publish videos there that will help you write better, be a better authorpreneur, and market your books.

In any case, visit me at www.authorlevelup.com.

I've taught you everything I know (again).

Now go write.

Peace, love, and light,
M.L. Ronn

Read Next: Mental Models for Writers

The world's smartest people use these secrets to 10x their success and make more money—and you can, too!

. . .

Do you wish you knew the unwritten rules to being a successful writer—you know, the things that no one will ever tell you?

Mental models are the unwritten rules of success.

Used in fields like science, engineering, and economics, mental models have guided important people for centuries...

It's only in the last few decades that these secrets have been "unmasked" by successful businessmen like Warren Buffet and Charlie Munger. But many people still don't know about them...

In this writer's guide, prolific writer M.L. Ronn taps into the mysterious world of mental models, frameworks for thinking that will revolutionize the way you approach every aspect of the writing life.

This is the only mental model book on the market written specifically for writers!
 • Win big with your writing by applying strange yet curiously effective ideas from mega thinkers like Plato, Sir Isaac Newton, and more
 • Solve every writing problem effortlessly (including writer's block!)
 • Collect unfair advantages in every area of the writing life, including creativity, fiction writing, and business
 • Transform your marketing & promotion using the laws of persuasion
 In today's new world of publishing, the world and all of its

riches belong to the writers who dare to elevate their thinking and blaze new paths.

Are you willing to learn what it takes to join the world's most successful writers and thinkers?

Get your copy of Mental Models for Writers today at www. authorlevelup.com/mentalmodels.

Meet M.L. Ronn

Science fiction and fantasy on the wild side!

M.L. Ronn (Michael La Ronn) is the author of many science fiction and fantasy novels including *The Good Necromancer*, *Android X*, and *The Last Dragon Lord* series.

In 2012, a life-threatening illness made him realize that storytelling was his #1 passion. He's devoted his life to writing ever since, making up whatever story makes him fall out of his chair laughing the hardest. Every day.

Learn more about Michael
www.authorlevelup.com (for writers)
www.michaellaronn.com (fiction)

More Books by M.L. Ronn

Books for Writers

Indie Author Confidential (Series)
How to Write Your First Novel
Be a Writing Machine
Mental Models for Writers
The Indie Writer's Encyclopedia
The Indie Author Atlas
The Indie Author Bestiary
The Reader's Bill of Rights
The Self-Publishing Compendium
150 Self-Publishing Questions Answered
Authors, Steal This Book
The Indie Author Strategy Guide
How to Dictate a Book
Advanced Author Editing
Keep Your Books Selling
The Author Estate Handbook
The Author Heir Handbook
Interactive Fiction: How to Engage Readers and Push the Boundaries of Story Telling

Indie Poet Rock Star
Indie Poet Formatting
2016 Indie Author State of the Union

More Books for Writers:

www.authorlevelup.com/books

Fiction:

www.michaellaronn.com/books

www.ingramcontent.com/pod-product-compliance
Lightning Source LLC
Chambersburg PA
CBHW020404130626
46549CB00006B/2435